Programming in Haskell

Graham Hutton

University of Nottingham

 CAMBRIDGE
UNIVERSITY PRESS

CAMBRIDGE UNIVERSITY PRESS
Cambridge, New York, Melbourne, Madrid, Cape Town, Singapore, São Paulo,
Delhi, Dubai, Tokyo

Cambridge University Press
The Edinburgh Building, Cambridge CB2 8RU, UK

Published in the United States of America by Cambridge University Press, New York

www.cambridge.org
Information on this title: www.cambridge.org/9780521692694

First published 2007
Sixth printing 2010

Printed in the United Kingdom at the University Press, Cambridge

A catalogue record for this publication is available from the British Library

Library of Congress Cataloguing in Publication data

ISBN 978-0-521-87172-3 hardback
ISBN 978-0-521-69269-4 paperback

Programming in Haskell

Haskell is one of the leading languages for teaching functional programming, enabling students to write simpler and cleaner code, and to learn how to structure and reason about programs.

This introduction is ideal for beginners: it requires no previous programming experience and all concepts are explained from first principles with the aid of carefully chosen examples. Each chapter includes a series of exercises, ranging from the straightforward to extended projects, along with suggestions for further reading on more advanced topics. The presentation is clear and simple, and benefits from having been refined and class-tested over several years.

Features:

- Powerpoint slides for each chapter freely available for instructors and students from the book's website
- Solutions to exercises, and examination questions (with solutions) available to instructors
- All the code in the book is fully compliant with the latest release of Haskell, and can be downloaded from the web.
- Written by a leading Haskell researcher and instructor, well known for his teaching skills
- Can be used with courses, or as a stand-alone text for self-learning

Graham Hutton has worked in four of the leading centres for research and teaching on functional programming. He has more than 15 years of experience in functional programming research, during which time he has published more than 30 research articles, chaired the Haskell Workshop, and edited a special issue on Haskell of the *Journal of Functional Programming*. He also has more than 10 years' experience in teaching Haskell, and in promoting the use of functional programming in the curriculum.

For Annette, Callum and Tom

Contents

Preface

... there are two ways of constructing a software design: One way is to make it so simple that there are *obviously* no deficiencies and the other way is to make it so complicated that there are no *obvious* deficiencies. The first method is far more difficult.

Tony Hoare, 1980 ACM Turing Award Lecture

This book is about an approach to programming in which simplicity, clarity, and elegance are the key goals. More specifically, it is an introduction to the functional style of programming, using the language Haskell.

The functional style is quite different to that promoted by most current languages, such as Java, C++, C, and Visual Basic. In particular, most current languages are closely linked to the underlying hardware, in the sense that programming is based upon the idea of changing stored values. In contrast, Haskell promotes a more abstract style of programming, based upon the idea of applying functions to arguments. As we shall see, moving to this higher-level leads to considerably simpler programs, and supports a number of powerful new ways to structure and reason about programs.

The book is primarily aimed at students studying computing science at university level, but is also appropriate for a broader spectrum of readers who would like to learn about programming in Haskell. No previous programming experience is required or assumed, and all the concepts are explained from first principles, with the aid of carefully chosen examples.

The version of Haskell used in the book is Haskell 98, the standard version of the language, for which the recently published definition is the culmination of fifteen years of work by its designers. As this is an introductory text, we do not attempt to cover all aspects of Haskell and its associated libraries. Around half of the book is dedicated to introducing the main features of the language, while the other half comprises examples and case studies of programming of Haskell. Each chapter includes a series of exercises, and suggestions for further reading on more advanced and specialist topics.

The book is based upon course material that has been refined and class-tested over many years at the University of Nottingham. Most of the material from the book can be covered in twenty hours of lectures, supported by approximately forty hours of private study, practical sessions in a supervised laboratory, and take-home programming courseworks. However, additional time would be required to cover some of the later chapters in more detail, along with some of the later programming examples.

The website for the book provides a range of supporting material, including Powerpoint slides for each chapter, and Haskell code for each of the extended examples. Instructors can also obtain model answers to the exercises for each chapter, together with a large collection of exam questions and their model answers, by emailing solutions@cambridge.org.

Acknowledgements

The Foundations of Programming group at the University of Nottingham is an excellent environment in which to do research and teaching on functional programming. I am grateful to the University for providing a sabbatical to start work on this book; all the students and tutors on my Haskell courses for their feedback; and Thorsten Altenkirch, Neil Ghani, Mark Jones (now at Portland State), Conor McBride, and Henrik Nilsson in the FOP group for our many discussions about functional ideas and how to present them.

I would also like to thank David Tranah and Dawn Preston for their editorial work at Cambridge University Press; Mark Jones for the Hugs interpreter for Haskell; Ralf Hinze and Andres Löh for the lhs2TeX system for typesetting Haskell; Rik van Geldrop and Jaap van der Woude for their feedback on using drafts of the book; Kees van den Broek, Frank Heitmann, and Bill Tonkin for pointing out errors; Ian Bayley and the anonymous reviewers for useful comments; and Joel Wright for timing the countdown programs.

Graham Hutton
Nottingham, 2006

chapter 1

Introduction

In this chapter we set the stage for the rest of the book. We start by reviewing the notion of a function, then introduce the concept of functional programming, summarise the main features of Haskell and its history, and conclude with two small examples that give a taste of Haskell.

1.1 | Functions

In Haskell, a *function* is a mapping that takes one or more arguments and produces a single result, and is defined using an equation that gives a name for the function, a name for each of its arguments, and a body that specifies how the result can be calculated in terms of the arguments.

For example, a function *double* that takes a number x as its argument, and produces the result $x + x$, can be defined by the following equation:

$$double\ x\ =\ x + x$$

When a function is applied to actual arguments, the result is obtained by substituting these arguments into the body of the function in place of the argument names. This process may immediately produce a result that cannot be further simplified, such as a number. More commonly, however, the result will be an expression containing other function applications, which must then be processed in the same way to produce the final result.

For example, the result of the application *double* 3 of the function *double* to the number 3 can be determined by the following calculation, in which each step is explained by a short comment in curly parentheses:

$$double\ 3$$
$$=\qquad \{ \text{applying } double \}$$
$$3 + 3$$
$$=\qquad \{ \text{applying } + \}$$
$$6$$

Similarly, the result of the nested application *double* (*double* 2) in which the function *double* is applied twice can be calculated as follows:

$$
\begin{aligned}
& double\ (double\ 2) \\
= &\quad \{ \text{applying the inner } double \} \\
& double\ (2 + 2) \\
= &\quad \{ \text{applying } + \} \\
& double\ 4 \\
= &\quad \{ \text{applying } double \} \\
& 4 + 4 \\
= &\quad \{ \text{applying } + \} \\
& 8
\end{aligned}
$$

Alternatively, the same result could also be calculated by starting with the outer application of the function *double* rather than the inner:

$$
\begin{aligned}
& double\ (double\ 2) \\
= &\quad \{ \text{applying the outer } double \} \\
& double\ 2 + double\ 2 \\
= &\quad \{ \text{applying the first } double \} \\
& (2 + 2) + double\ 2 \\
= &\quad \{ \text{applying the first } + \} \\
& 4 + double\ 2 \\
= &\quad \{ \text{applying } double \} \\
& 4 + (2 + 2) \\
= &\quad \{ \text{applying the second } + \} \\
& 4 + 4 \\
= &\quad \{ \text{applying } + \} \\
& 8
\end{aligned}
$$

However, this calculation requires two more steps than our original version, because the expression *double* 2 is duplicated in the first step and hence simplified twice. In general, the order in which functions are applied in a calculation does not affect the value of the final result, but it may affect the number of steps required, and may affect whether the calculation process terminates. These issues are explored in more detail in chapter 12.

1.2 | Functional programming

What is functional programming? Opinions differ, and it is difficult to give a precise definition. Generally speaking, however, functional programming can be viewed as a *style* of programming in which the basic method of computation is the application of functions to arguments. In turn, a functional programming language is one that *supports* and *encourages* the functional style.

To illustrate these ideas, let us consider the task of computing the sum of the integers (whole numbers) between one and some larger number n. In most current programming languages, this would normally be achieved using two variables that store values that can be changed over time, one such variable used to count up to n, and the other used to accumulate the total.

For example, if we use the assignment symbol := to change the value of a variable, and the keywords **repeat** and **until** to repeatedly execute a sequence of instructions until a condition is satisfied, then the following sequence of instructions computes the required sum:

$$count := 0$$
$$total := 0$$
repeat
$$\quad count := count + 1$$
$$\quad total := total + count$$
until
$$\quad count = n$$

That is, we first initialise both the counter and the total to zero, and then repeatedly increment the counter and add this value to the total until the counter reaches n, at which point the computation stops.

In the above program, the basic method of computation is changing stored values, in the sense that executing the program results in a sequence of assignments. For example, the case of $n = 5$ gives the following sequence, in which the final value assigned to the variable $total$ is the required sum:

$$
\begin{array}{lll}
count & := & 0 \\
total & := & 0 \\
count & := & 1 \\
total & := & 1 \\
count & := & 2 \\
total & := & 3 \\
count & := & 3 \\
total & := & 6 \\
count & := & 4 \\
total & := & 10 \\
count & := & 5 \\
total & := & 15 \\
\end{array}
$$

In general, programming languages in which the basic method of computation is changing stored values are called *imperative* languages, because programs in such languages are constructed from imperative instructions that specify precisely how the computation should proceed.

Now let us consider computing the sum of the numbers between one and n using Haskell. This would normally be achieved using two library functions, one called [..] used to produce the list of numbers between one and n, and the other called sum used to produce the sum of this list:

$$sum\ [1 .. n]$$

In this program, the basic method of computation is applying functions to arguments, in the sense that executing the program results in a sequence of applications. For example, the case of $n = 5$ gives the following sequence, in which the final result is the required sum:

$$sum\ [1 .. 5]$$
$$=\qquad \{\ \text{applying}\ [\ ..\ ]\ \}$$

$$
\begin{aligned}
& \quad sum\ [1, 2, 3, 4, 5] \\
=& \quad \{\text{applying } sum\ \} \\
& \quad 1 + 2 + 3 + 4 + 5 \\
=& \quad \{\text{applying } +\ \} \\
& \quad 15
\end{aligned}
$$

Most imperative languages support some form of programming with functions, so the Haskell program $sum\ [1 \mathinner{\ldotp\ldotp} n]$ could be translated into such languages. However, most imperative languages do not *encourage* programming in the functional style. For example, many languages discourage or prohibit functions from being stored in data structures such as lists, from constructing intermediate structures such as the list of numbers in the above example, from taking functions as arguments or producing functions as results, or from being defined in terms of themselves. In contrast, Haskell imposes no such restrictions on how functions can be used, and provides a range of features to make programming with functions both simple and powerful.

1.3 | Features of Haskell

For reference, the main features of Haskell are listed below, along with the particular chapters of this book that give further details.

- **Concise programs** (chapters 2 and 4)

  Due to the high-level nature of the functional style, programs written in Haskell are often much more *concise* than in other languages, as illustrated by the example in the previous section. Moreover, the syntax of Haskell has been designed with concise programs in mind, in particular by having few keywords, and by allowing indentation to be used to indicate the structure of programs. Although it is difficult to make an objective comparison, Haskell programs are often between two and ten times shorter than programs written in other current languages.

- **Powerful type system** (chapters 3 and 10)

  Most modern programming languages include some form of *type system* to detect incompatibility errors, such as attempting to add a number and a character. Haskell has a type system that requires little type information from the programmer, but allows a large class of incompatibility errors in programs to be automatically detected prior to their execution, using a sophisticated process called type inference. The Haskell type system is also more powerful than most current languages, by allowing functions to be "polymorphic" and "overloaded".

- **List comprehensions** (chapter 5)

  One of the most common ways to structure and manipulate data in computing is using lists. To this end, Haskell provides lists as a basic concept in the language, together with a simple but powerful *comprehension* notation that constructs new lists by selecting and filtering elements from one or more existing lists. Using the comprehension notation allows many common functions on lists to be defined in a clear and concise manner, without the need for explicit recursion.

- **Recursive functions** (chapter 6)
  Most non-trivial programs involve some form of repetition or looping. In Haskell, the basic mechanism by which looping is achieved is by using *recursive* functions that are defined in terms of themselves. Many computations have a simple and natural definition in terms of recursive functions, particularly when "pattern matching" and "guards" are used to separate different cases into different equations.

- **Higher-order functions** (chapter 7)
  Haskell is a *higher-order* functional language, which means that functions can freely take functions as arguments and produce functions as results. Using higher-order functions allows common programming patterns, such as composing two functions, to be defined as functions within the language itself. More generally, higher-order functions can be used to define "domain-specific languages" within Haskell, such as for list processing, parsing, and interactive programming.

- **Monadic effects** (chapters 8 and 9)
  Functions in Haskell are pure functions that take all their input as arguments and produce all their output as results. However, many programs require some form of *side effect* that would appear to be at odds with purity, such as reading input from the keyboard, or writing output to the screen, while the program is running. Haskell provides a uniform framework for handling effects without compromising the purity of functions, based upon the mathematical notion of a *monad*.

- **Lazy evaluation** (chapter 12)
  Haskell programs are executed using a technique called *lazy evaluation*, which is based upon the idea that no computation should be performed until its result is actually required. As well as avoiding unnecessary computation, lazy evaluation ensures that programs terminate whenever possible, encourages programming in a modular style using intermediate data structures, and even allows data structures with an infinite number of elements, such as an infinite list of numbers.

- **Reasoning about programs** (chapter 13)
  Because programs in Haskell are pure functions, simple *equational reasoning* can be used to execute programs, to transform programs, to prove properties of programs, and even to derive programs directly from specifications of their behaviour. Equational reasoning is particularly powerful when combined with the use of "induction" to reason about functions that are defined using recursion.

1.4 | Historical background

Many of the features of Haskell are not new, but were first introduced by other languages. To help place Haskell in context, some of the main historical developments related to the language are briefly summarised below:

- In the 1930s, Alonzo Church developed the lambda calculus, a simple but powerful mathematical theory of functions.

- In the 1950s, John McCarthy developed Lisp ("LISt Processor"), generally regarded as being the first functional programming language. Lisp had some influences from the lambda calculus, but still adopted variable assignments as a central feature of the language.

- In the 1960s, Peter Landin developed ISWIM ("If you See What I Mean"), the first pure functional programming language, based strongly on the lambda calculus and having no variable assignments.

- In the 1970s, John Backus developed FP ("Functional Programming"), a functional programming language that particularly emphasised the idea of higher-order functions and reasoning about programs.

- Also in the 1970s, Robin Milner and others developed ML ("Meta-Language"), the first of the modern functional programming languages, which introduced the idea of polymorphic types and type inference.

- In the 1970s and 1980s, David Turner developed a number of lazy functional programming languages, culminating in the commercially produced language Miranda (meaning "admirable").

- In 1987, an international committee of researchers initiated the development of Haskell (named after the logician Haskell Curry), a standard lazy functional programming language.

- In 2003, the committee published the Haskell Report, which defines a long-awaited stable version of Haskell, and is the culmination of fifteen years of work on the language by its designers.

It is worthy of note that three of the above researchers — McCarthy, Backus, and Milner — have each received the ACM Turing Award, which is generally regarded as being the computing equivalent of a Nobel prize.

1.5 | A taste of Haskell

We conclude this chapter with two small examples that give a taste of programming in Haskell. First of all, recall the function *sum* used earlier in this chapter, which produces the sum of a list of numbers. In Haskell, this function can be defined using the following two equations:

$$
\begin{aligned}
sum\ [\,] &= 0 \\
sum\ (x : xs) &= x + sum\ xs
\end{aligned}
$$

The first equation states that the sum of the empty list is zero, while the second states that the sum of any non-empty list comprising a first number x and a remaining list of numbers xs is given by adding x and the sum of xs. For example, the result of $sum\ [1, 2, 3]$ can be calculated as follows:

$$
\begin{aligned}
&\quad sum\ [1, 2, 3] \\
&=\quad \{\text{applying } sum\ \} \\
&\quad 1 + sum\ [2, 3] \\
&=\quad \{\text{applying } sum\ \} \\
&\quad 1 + (2 + sum\ [3]) \\
&=\quad \{\text{applying } sum\ \} \\
&\quad 1 + (2 + (3 + sum\ [\,])) \\
&=\quad \{\text{applying } sum\ \} \\
&\quad 1 + (2 + (3 + 0)) \\
&=\quad \{\text{applying } + \} \\
&\quad 6
\end{aligned}
$$

Note that even though the function sum is defined in terms of itself and is hence recursive, it does not loop forever. In particular, each application of sum reduces the length of the argument list by one, until the list eventually becomes empty, at which point the recursion stops. Returning zero as the sum of the empty list is appropriate because zero is the *identity* for addition. That is, $0 + x = x$ and $x + 0 = x$ for any number x.

In Haskell, every function has a *type* that specifies the nature of its arguments and results, which is automatically inferred from the definition of the function. For example, the function sum has the following type:

$$
Num\ a \Rightarrow [a] \to a
$$

This type states that for any type a of numbers, sum is a function that maps a list of such numbers to a single such number. Haskell supports many different types of numbers, including integers such as 123, and "floating-point" numbers such as 3.14159. Hence, for example, sum could be applied to a list of integers, as in the calculation above, or to a list of floating-point numbers.

Types provide useful information about the nature of functions, but, more importantly, their use allows many errors in programs to be automatically detected prior to executing the programs themselves. In particular, for every function application in a program, a check is made that the type of the actual arguments is compatible with the type of the function itself. For example, attempting to apply the function sum to a list of characters would be reported as an error, because characters are not a type of numbers.

Now let us consider a more interesting function concerning lists, which illustrates a number of other aspects of Haskell. Suppose that we define a function called $qsort$ by the following two equations:

$$qsort\;[\,] \quad\quad = \quad [\,]$$
$$qsort\;(x:xs) \quad = \quad qsort\;smaller \mathbin{+\!\!+} [\,x\,] \mathbin{+\!\!+} qsort\;larger$$
$$\textbf{where}$$
$$smaller = [\,a \mid a \leftarrow xs,\, a \leq x\,]$$
$$larger = [\,b \mid b \leftarrow xs,\, b > x\,]$$

In this definition, $\mathbin{+\!\!+}$ is an operator that appends two lists; for example, $[1, 2, 3] \mathbin{+\!\!+} [4, 5] = [1, 2, 3, 4, 5]$. In turn, **where** is a keyword that introduces local definitions, in this case a list *smaller* that consists of all elements a from the list xs that are less than or equal to x, together with a list *larger* that consists of all elements b from xs that are greater than x. For example, if $x = 3$ and $xs = [5, 1, 4, 2]$, then $smaller = [1, 2]$ and $larger = [5, 4]$.

What does *qsort* actually do? First of all, we show that it has no effect on lists with a single element, in the sense that $qsort\;[\,x\,] = [\,x\,]$ for any x:

$$qsort\;[\,x\,]$$
$$= \quad \{\,\text{applying } qsort \,\}$$
$$qsort\;[\,] \mathbin{+\!\!+} [\,x\,] \mathbin{+\!\!+} qsort\;[\,]$$
$$= \quad \{\,\text{applying } qsort \,\}$$
$$[\,] \mathbin{+\!\!+} [\,x\,] \mathbin{+\!\!+} [\,]$$
$$= \quad \{\,\text{applying } \mathbin{+\!\!+} \,\}$$
$$[\,x\,]$$

In turn, we now work through the application of *qsort* to an example list, using the above property to simplify the calculation:

$$qsort\;[3, 5, 1, 4, 2]$$
$$= \quad \{\,\text{applying } qsort \,\}$$
$$qsort\;[1, 2] \mathbin{+\!\!+} [3] \mathbin{+\!\!+} qsort\;[5, 4]$$
$$= \quad \{\,\text{applying } qsort \,\}$$
$$(qsort\;[\,] \mathbin{+\!\!+} [1] \mathbin{+\!\!+} qsort\;[2]) \mathbin{+\!\!+} [3]$$
$$\mathbin{+\!\!+} (qsort\;[4] \mathbin{+\!\!+} [5] \mathbin{+\!\!+} qsort\;[\,])$$
$$= \quad \{\,\text{applying } qsort, \text{above property} \,\}$$
$$([\,] \mathbin{+\!\!+} [1] \mathbin{+\!\!+} [2]) \mathbin{+\!\!+} [3] \mathbin{+\!\!+} ([4] \mathbin{+\!\!+} [5] \mathbin{+\!\!+} [\,])$$
$$= \quad \{\,\text{applying } \mathbin{+\!\!+} \,\}$$
$$[1, 2] \mathbin{+\!\!+} [3] \mathbin{+\!\!+} [4, 5]$$
$$= \quad \{\,\text{applying } \mathbin{+\!\!+} \,\}$$
$$[1, 2, 3, 4, 5]$$

In summary, *qsort* has sorted the example list into numerical order. More generally, this function produces a sorted version of any list of numbers. The first equation for *qsort* states that the empty list is already sorted, while the second states that any non-empty list can be sorted by inserting the first number between the two lists that result from sorting the remaining numbers that are *smaller* and *larger* than this number. This method of sorting is called *quicksort*, and is one of the best such methods known.

The above implementation of quicksort is an excellent example of the power of Haskell, being both clear and concise. Moreover, the function *qsort* is also more general than might be expected, being applicable not just with numbers, but with any type of ordered values. More precisely, the type

$$qsort \quad :: \quad Ord\ a \Rightarrow [\,a\,] \rightarrow [\,a\,]$$

states that, for any type a of ordered values, $qsort$ is a function that maps between lists of such values. Haskell supports many different types of ordered values, including numbers, single characters such as $'a'$, and strings of characters such as `"abcde"`. Hence, for example, the function $qsort$ could also be used to sort a list of characters, or a list of strings.

1.6 | Chapter remarks

The Haskell Report is freely available on the web from the Haskell home page, *www.haskell.org*, and has also been published as a book (25). A more detailed historical account of the development of functional programming languages is given in Hudak's survey article (11).

1.7 | Exercises

1. Give another possible calculation for the result of $double\ (double\ 2)$.

2. Show that $sum\ [x] = x$ for any number x.

3. Define a function $product$ that produces the product of a list of numbers, and show using your definition that $product\ [2, 3, 4] = 24$.

4. How should the definition of the function $qsort$ be modified so that it produces a *reverse* sorted version of a list?

5. What would be the effect of replacing $\leq$ by $<$ in the definition of $qsort$? Hint: consider the example $qsort\ [2, 2, 3, 1, 1]$.

chapter 2

First steps

In this chapter we take our first proper steps with Haskell. We start by introducing the Hugs system and the standard prelude, then explain the notation for function application, develop our first Haskell script, and conclude by discussing a number of syntactic conventions concerning scripts.

2.1 | The Hugs system

As we saw in the previous chapter, small Haskell programs can be executed by hand. In practice, however, we usually require a system that can execute programs automatically. In this book we use an interactive system called *Hugs*, which is the most widely used implementation of Haskell.

The interactive nature of Hugs makes it well suited for teaching and prototyping, and its performance is sufficient for most applications. However, if greater performance or a stand-alone executable version of a program is required, a number of compilers for Haskell are also available, of which the most widely used is the Glasgow Haskell Compiler. This compiler also has an interactive version that operates in a similar manner to Hugs, and can readily be used in its place for the purposes of this book.

2.2 | The standard prelude

When the Hugs system is started it first loads a library file called *Prelude.hs*, and then displays a > prompt to indicate that the system is waiting for the user to enter an expression to be evaluated. For example, the library file defines many familiar functions that operate on integers, including the five main arithmetic operations of addition, subtraction, multiplication, division, and exponentiation, as illustrated below:

> `> 2 + 3`

5

```
> 2 − 3
−1

> 2 ∗ 3
6

> 7 'div' 2
3

> 2 ↑ 3
8
```

Note that the integer division operator is written as '*div*', and rounds down to the nearest integer if the result is a proper fraction.

Following normal mathematical convention, exponentiation has higher priority than multiplication and division, which in turn have higher priority than addition and subtraction. For example, $2 * 3 \uparrow 4$ means $2 * (3 \uparrow 4)$, while $2 + 3 * 4$ means $2 + (3 * 4)$. Moreover, exponentiation associates (brackets) to the right, while the other four arithmetic operators associate to the left. For example, $2 \uparrow 3 \uparrow 4$ means $2 \uparrow (3 \uparrow 4)$, while $2 - 3 + 4$ means $(2 - 3) + 4$. In practice, however, it is often clearer to use explicit parentheses in such arithmetic expressions, rather than relying on the above conventions.

In addition to functions on integers, the library file also provides a range of useful functions that operate on lists. In Haskell, the elements of a list are enclosed in square parentheses, and are separated by commas. Some of the most commonly used library functions on lists are illustrated below.

- Select the first element of a non-empty list:

  ```
  > head [1, 2, 3, 4, 5]
  1
  ```

- Remove the first element from a non-empty list:

  ```
  > tail [1, 2, 3, 4, 5]
  [2, 3, 4, 5]
  ```

- Select the nth element of list (counting from zero):

  ```
  > [1, 2, 3, 4, 5] !! 2
  3
  ```

- Select the first n elements of a list:

  ```
  > take 3 [1, 2, 3, 4, 5]
  [1, 2, 3]
  ```

- Remove the first n elements from a list:

  ```
  > drop 3 [1, 2, 3, 4, 5]
  [4, 5]
  ```

- Calculate the length of a list:

  > *length* $[1, 2, 3, 4, 5]$
  5

- Calculate the sum of a list of numbers:

  > *sum* $[1, 2, 3, 4, 5]$
  15

- Calculate the product of a list of numbers:

  > *product* $[1, 2, 3, 4, 5]$
  120

- Append two lists:

  > $[1, 2, 3]$ ++ $[4, 5]$
  $[1, 2, 3, 4, 5]$

- Reverse a list:

  > *reverse* $[1, 2, 3, 4, 5]$
  $[5, 4, 3, 2, 1]$

Some of the functions in the standard prelude may produce an error for certain values of their arguments. For example, attempting to divide by zero or select the first element of an empty list will produce an error:

> 1 'div' 0
Error

> *head* $[\,]$
Error

In practice, when an error occurs the Hugs system also produces a message that provides some information about the likely cause.

For reference, appendix A presents some of the most commonly used definitions from the standard prelude, and appendix B shows how special Haskell symbols, such as ↑ and ++, are typed using a normal keyboard.

2.3 | Function application

In mathematics, the application of a function to its arguments is usually denoted by enclosing the arguments in parentheses, while the multiplication of two values is often denoted silently, by writing the two values next to one another. For example, in mathematics the expression

$$f(a, b) + c\ d$$

means apply the function f to two arguments a and b, and add the result to the product of c and d. Reflecting its primary status in the language, function application in Haskell is denoted silently using spacing, while the multiplication of two values is denoted explicitly using the operator $*$. For example, the expression above would be written in Haskell as follows:

$$f \ a \ b + c * d$$

Moreover, function application has higher priority than all other operators. For example, $f \ a + b$ means $(f \ a) + b$. The following table gives a few further examples to illustrate the differences between the notation for function application in mathematics and in Haskell:

Mathematics	Haskell
$f(x)$	$f \ x$
$f(x, y)$	$f \ x \ y$
$f(g(x))$	$f \ (g \ x)$
$f(x, g(y))$	$f \ x \ (g \ y)$
$f(x)g(y)$	$f \ x * g \ y$

Note that parentheses are still required in the Haskell expression $f \ (g \ x)$ above, because $f \ g \ x$ on its own would be interpreted as the application of the function f to two arguments g and x, whereas the intention is that f is applied to one argument, namely the result of applying the function g to an argument x. A similar remark holds for the expression $f \ x \ (g \ y)$.

2.4 | Haskell scripts

As well as the functions provided in the standard prelude, it is also possible to define new functions. New functions cannot be defined at the > prompt within Hugs, but must be defined within a *script*, a text file comprising a sequence of definitions. By convention, Haskell scripts usually have a *.hs* suffix on their filename to differentiate them from other kinds of files.

My first script

When developing a Haskell script, it is useful to keep two windows open, one running an editor for the script, and the other running Hugs. As an example, suppose that we start a text editor and type in the following two function definitions, and save the script to a file called *test.hs*:

```
double x     =  x + x
quadruple x  =  double (double x)
```

In turn, suppose that we leave the editor open, and in another window start up the Hugs system and instruct it to load the new script:

```
> :load test.hs
```

Now both *Prelude.hs* and *test.hs* are loaded, and functions from both scripts can be freely used. For example:

```
> quadruple 10
40
```

```
> take (double 2) [1, 2, 3, 4, 5, 6]
[1, 2, 3, 4]
```

Now suppose that we leave Hugs open, return to the editor, add the following two function definitions to those already typed in, and then resave the file:

$$factorial\ n\ =\ product\ [1 .. n]$$
$$average\ ns\ =\ sum\ ns\ `div`\ length\ ns$$

We could equally well have defined *average ns = div (sum ns) (length ns)*, but writing *div* between its two arguments is more natural. In general, any function with two arguments can be written between its arguments by enclosing the name of the function in single back quotes ' '.

Hugs does not automatically reload scripts when they are modified, so a reload command must be executed before the new definitions can be used:

```
> :reload
```

```
> factorial 10
3628800
```

```
> average [1, 2, 3, 4, 5]
3
```

For reference, the table below summarises the meaning of some of the most commonly used Hugs commands. Note that any command can be abbreviated by its first character. For example, :*load* can be abbreviated by :*l*. The command :*type* is explained in more detail in the next chapter.

Command	Meaning
:*load name*	load script *name*
:*reload*	reload current script
:*edit name*	edit script *name*
:*edit*	edit current script
:*type expr*	show type of *expr*
:?	show all commands
:*quit*	quit Hugs

Naming requirements

When defining a new function, the names of the function and its arguments must begin with a lower-case letter, but can then be followed by zero or more letters (both lower- and upper-case), digits, underscores, and forward single quotes. For example, the following are all valid names:

$$myFun \quad fun1 \quad arg\_2 \quad x'$$

The following list of *keywords* have a special meaning in the language, and cannot be used as the names of functions or their arguments:

case	**class**	**data**	**default**	**deriving**	**do**	**else**
if	**import**	**in**	**infix**	**infixl**	**infixr**	**instance**
let	**module**	**newtype**	**of**	**then**	**type**	**where**

By convention, list arguments in Haskell usually have the suffix s on their name to indicate that they may contain multiple values. For example, a list of numbers might be named ns, a list of arbitrary values might be named xs, and a list of list of characters might be named css.

The layout rule

Within a script, each definition must begin in precisely the same column. This *layout rule* makes it possible to determine the grouping of definitions from their indentation. For example, in the script

$$
\begin{aligned}
a \;=\; & b + c \\
& \mathbf{where} \\
& \quad b = 1 \\
& \quad c = 2 \\
d \;=\; & a * 2
\end{aligned}
$$

it is clear from the indentation that b and c are local definitions for use within the body of a. If desired, such grouping can be made explicit by enclosing a sequence of definitions in curly parentheses and separating each definition by a semi-colon. For example, the above script could also be written as:

$$
\begin{aligned}
a = \;& b + c \\
& \mathbf{where} \\
& \quad \{\, b = 1; \\
& \quad\quad c = 2\} \\
d = \;& a * 2
\end{aligned}
$$

In general, however, it is usually clearer to rely on the layout rule to determine the grouping of definitions, rather than use explicit syntax.

Comments

In addition to new definitions, scripts can also contain comments that will be ignored by Hugs. Haskell provides two kinds of comments, called *ordinary* and *nested*. Ordinary comments begin with the symbol -- and extend to the end of the current line, as in the following examples:

```
-- Factorial of a positive integer:
```
$$factorial\ n \;=\; product\,[\,1\mathbin{..} n\,]$$
```
-- Average of a list of integers:
```
$$average\ ns \;=\; sum\ ns\ `div`\ length\ ns$$

Nested comments begin and end with the symbols {- and -}, may span multiple lines, and may be nested in the sense that comments can contain other comments. Nested comments are particularly useful for temporarily removing sections of definitions from a script, as in the following example:

```
{-
double x     =   x + x
quadruple x  =   double (double x)
-}
```

2.5 | Chapter remarks

The Hugs system is freely available on the web from the Haskell home page, *www.haskell.org*, which also contains a wealth of other useful resources.

2.6 | Exercises

1. Parenthesise the following arithmetic expressions:

   $2 \uparrow 3 * 4$

   $2 * 3 + 4 * 5$

   $2 + 3 * 4 \uparrow 5$

2. Work through the examples from this chapter using Hugs.

3. The script below contains three syntactic errors. Correct these errors and then check that your script works properly using Hugs.

   N $=$ a `div` $length\ xs$
        where
          $a = 10$
         $xs = [1, 2, 3, 4, 5]$

4. Show how the library function *last* that selects the last element of a non-empty list could be defined in terms of the library functions introduced in this chapter. Can you think of another possible definition?

5. Show how the library function *init* that removes the last element from a non-empty list could similarly be defined in two different ways.

chapter 3

Types and classes

In this chapter we introduce types and classes, two of the most fundamental concepts in Haskell. We start by explaining what types are and how they are used in Haskell, then present a number of basic types and ways to build larger types by combining smaller types, discuss function types in more detail, and conclude with the concepts of polymorphic types and type classes.

3.1 | Basic concepts

A *type* is a collection of related values. For example, the type *Bool* contains the two logical values *False* and *True*, while the type *Bool* → *Bool* contains all functions that map arguments from *Bool* to results from *Bool*, such as the logical negation function ¬. We use the notation $v :: T$ to mean that v is a value in the type T, and say that v "has type" T. For example:

$$
\begin{aligned}
False &:: Bool \\
True &:: Bool \\
\neg &:: Bool \to Bool
\end{aligned}
$$

More generally, the symbol :: can also be used with expressions that have not yet been evaluated, in which case $e :: T$ means that evaluation of the expression e will produce a value of type T. For example:

$$
\begin{aligned}
\neg\, False &:: Bool \\
\neg\, True &:: Bool \\
\neg\,(\neg\, False) &:: Bool
\end{aligned}
$$

In Haskell, every expression must have a type, which is calculated prior to evaluating the expression by a process called *type inference*. The key to this process is a typing rule for function application, which states that if f is a function that maps arguments of type A to results of type B, and e is an expression of type A, then the application $f\ e$ has type B:

$$\frac{f :: A \to B \qquad e :: A}{f \ e :: B}$$

For example, the typing $\neg$ *False* :: *Bool* can be inferred from this rule using the fact that $\neg$ :: *Bool* $\to$ *Bool* and *False* :: *Bool*. On the other hand, the expression $\neg$ 3 does not have a type under the above rule for function application, because this would require that 3 :: *Bool*, which is not valid because 3 is not a logical value. Expressions such as $\neg$ 3 that do not have a type are said to contain a type error, and are deemed to be invalid expressions.

Because type inference precedes evaluation, Haskell programs are *type safe*, in the sense that type errors can never occur during evaluation. In practice, type inference detects a very large class of program errors, and is one of the most useful features of Haskell. Note, however, that the use of type inference does not eliminate the possibility that other kinds of error may occur during evaluation. For example, the expression 1 '*div*' 0 is free from type errors, but produces an error when evaluated because division by zero is undefined.

The downside of type safety is that some expressions that evaluate successfully will be rejected on type grounds. For example, the conditional expression **if** *True* **then** 1 **else** *False* evaluates to the number 1, but contains a type error and is hence deemed invalid. In particular, the typing rule for a conditional expression requires that both possible results have the same type, whereas in this case the first such result, 1, is a number and the second, *False*, is a logical value. In practice, however, programmers quickly learn how to work within the limits of the type system and avoid such problems.

In Hugs, the type of any expression can be displayed by preceding the expression by the command :*type*. For example:

```
> :type ¬
¬ :: Bool → Bool

> :type ¬ False
¬ False :: Bool

> :type ¬ 3
Error
```

3.2 | Basic types

Haskell provides a number of basic types that are built-in to the language, of which the most commonly used are described below.

Bool – logical values
This type contains the two logical values *False* and *True*.

Char – single characters
This type contains all single characters that are available from a normal keyboard, such as 'a', 'A', '3' and '_', as well as a number of control char-

acters that have a special effect, such as ' \n' (move to a new line) and ' \t' (move to the next tab stop). As is standard in most programming languages, single characters must be enclosed in single forward quotes ' '.

String – strings of characters

This type contains all sequences of characters, such as "abc", "1+2=3", and the empty string "". Again, as is standard in most programming languages, strings of characters must be enclosed in double quotes " ".

Int – fixed-precision integers

This type contains integers such as -100, 0, and 999, with a fixed amount of computer memory being used for their storage. For example, the Hugs system has values of type *Int* in the range -2^{31} to $2^{31} - 1$. Going outside this range can give unexpected results. For example, evaluating $2 \uparrow 31 :: Int$ using Hugs (the use of :: forces the result to an *Int* rather than some other numeric type) gives a negative number as the result, which is incorrect.

Integer – arbitrary-precision integers

This type contains all integers, with as much memory as necessary being used for their storage, thus avoiding the imposition of lower and upper limits on the range of numbers. For example, evaluating $2 \uparrow 31 :: Integer$ using any Haskell system will produce the correct result.

Apart from the different memory requirements and precision for numbers of type *Int* and *Integer*, the choice between these two types is also one of performance. In particular, most computers have built-in hardware for processing fixed-precision integers, whereas arbitrary-precision integers must usually be processed using the slower medium of software, as sequences of digits.

Float – single-precision floating-point numbers

This type contains numbers with a decimal point, such as -12.34, 1.0, and 3.14159, with a fixed amount of memory being used for their storage. The term *floating-point* comes from the fact that the number of digits permitted after the decimal point depends upon the magnitude of the number. For example, evaluating $sqrt\ 2 :: Float$ using Hugs gives the result 1.41421 (the library function *sqrt* calculates the square root of a number), which has five digits after the point, whereas $sqrt\ 99999 :: Float$ gives 316.226, which only has three digits after the point. Programming with floating-point numbers is a specialist topic that requires a careful treatment of rounding errors, and we say little more about such numbers in this introductory text.

We conclude this section by noting a single number may have more than one numeric type. For example, $3 :: Int$, $3 :: Integer$, and $3 :: Float$ are all valid typings for the number 3. This raises the interesting question of what type such numbers should be assigned during type inference, which will be answered later in this chapter when we consider type classes.

3.3 | List types

A *list* is a sequence of *elements* of the same type, with the elements being enclosed in square parentheses and separated by commas. We write [*T*] for the type of all lists whose elements have type *T*. For example:

[*False*, *True*, *False*]	::	[*Bool*]
['a', 'b', 'c', 'd']	::	[*Char*]
["One", "Two", "Three"]	::	[*String*]

The number of elements in a list is called its *length*. The list [ ] of length zero is called the empty list, while lists of length one, such as such as [*False*] and ['a'], are called singleton lists. Note that [[ ]] and [ ] are different lists, the former being a singleton list comprising the empty list as its only element, and the latter being simply the empty list.

There are three further points to note about list types. First of all, the type of a list conveys no information about its length. For example, the lists [*False*, *True*] and [*False*, *True*, *False*] both have type [*Bool*], even though they have different lengths. Secondly, there are no restrictions on the type of the elements of a list. At present we are limited in the range of examples that we can give because the only non-basic type that we have introduced at this point is list types, but we can have lists of lists, such as:

[['a', 'b'], ['c', 'd', 'e']] :: [[*Char*]]

Finally, there is no restriction that a list must have a finite length. In particular, due to the use of lazy evaluation in Haskell, lists with an infinite length are both natural and practical, as we shall see in chapter 12.

3.4 | Tuple types

A *tuple* is a finite sequence of *components* of possibly different types, with the components being enclosed in round parentheses and separated by commas. We write $(T_1, T_2, \ldots, T_n)$ for the type of all tuples whose ith components have type T_i for any i in the range 1 to n. For example:

(*False*, *True*)	::	(*Bool*, *Bool*)
(*False*, 'a', *True*)	::	(*Bool*, *Char*, *Bool*)
("Yes", *True*, 'a')	::	(*String*, *Bool*, *Char*)

The number of components in a tuple is called its *arity*. The tuple () of arity zero is called the empty tuple, tuples of arity two are called pairs, tuples of arity three are called triples, and so on. Tuples of arity one, such as (*False*), are not permitted because they would conflict with the use of parentheses to make the evaluation order explicit, such as in $(1 + 2) * 3$.

As with list types, there are three further points to note about tuple types. First of all, the type of a tuple conveys its arity. For example, the type (*Bool*, *Char*) contains all pairs comprising a first component of type *Bool* and a second component of type *Char*. Secondly, there are no restrictions on the types of the components of a tuple. For example, we can now have tuples of tuples, tuples of lists, and lists of tuples:

$$('\texttt{a}',(False,'\texttt{b}')) \qquad\quad :: \quad (Char,(Bool,Char))$$
$$(['\texttt{a}','\texttt{b}'],[False,True]) \quad :: \quad ([Char],[Bool])$$
$$[('\texttt{a}',False),('\texttt{b}',True)] \quad :: \quad [(Char,Bool)]$$

Finally, note that tuples must have a finite arity, in order to ensure that tuple types can always be calculated prior to evaluation.

3.5 | Function types

A *function* is a mapping from arguments of one type to results of another type. We write $T1 \rightarrow T2$ for the type of all functions that map arguments of type $T1$ to results of type $T2$. For example:

$$\neg \qquad :: \quad Bool \rightarrow Bool$$
$$isDigit \quad :: \quad Char \rightarrow Bool$$

(The library function $isDigit$ decides if a character is a numeric digit.) Because there are no restrictions on the types of the arguments and results of a function, the simple notion of a function with a single argument and result is already sufficient to handle multiple arguments and results, by packaging multiple values using lists or tuples. For example, we can define a function add that calculates the sum of a pair of integers, and a function $zeroto$ that returns the list of integers from zero to a given limit, as follows:

$$add \qquad\quad :: \quad (Int, Int) \rightarrow Int$$
$$add\ (x,y) \quad = \quad x+y$$
$$zeroto \qquad :: \quad Int \rightarrow [Int]$$
$$zeroto\ n \quad = \quad [0..n]$$

In these examples we have followed the Haskell convention of preceding function definitions by their types, which serves as useful documentation. Any such types provided manually by the user are checked for consistency with the types calculated automatically using type inference.

Note that there is no restriction that functions must be *total* on their argument type, in the sense that there may be some arguments for which the result is not defined. For example, the result of the library function $head$ that selects the first element of a list is undefined if the list is empty.

3.6 | Curried functions

Functions with multiple arguments can also be handled in another, perhaps less obvious way, by exploiting the fact that functions are free to return functions as results. For example, consider the following definition:

$$add' \qquad\quad :: \quad Int \rightarrow (Int \rightarrow Int)$$
$$add'\ x\ y \quad = \quad x+y$$

The type states that add' is a function that takes an argument of type Int, and returns a result that is a function of type $Int \to Int$. The definition itself states that add' takes an integer x followed by an integer y, and returns the result $x + y$. More precisely, add' takes an integer x and returns a function, which in turn takes an integer y and returns the result $x + y$.

Note that the function add' produces the same final result as the function add from the previous section, but whereas add takes its two arguments at the same time packaged as a pair, add' takes its two arguments one at a time, as reflected in the different types of the two functions:

$$add \quad :: \quad (Int, Int) \to Int$$
$$add' \quad :: \quad Int \to (Int \to Int)$$

Functions with more than two arguments can also be handled using the same technique, by returning functions that return functions, and so on. For example, a function $mult$ that takes three integers, one at a time, and returns their product, can be defined as follows:

$$mult \qquad :: \quad Int \to (Int \to (Int \to Int))$$
$$mult \; x \; y \; z \quad = \quad x * y * z$$

This definition states that $mult$ takes an integer x and returns a function, which in turn takes an integer y and returns another function, which finally takes an integer z and returns the result $x * y * z$.

Functions such as add' and $mult$ that take their arguments one at a time are called *curried*. As well as being interesting in their own right, curried functions are also more flexible than functions on tuples, because useful functions can often be made by *partially applying* a curried function with less than its full complement of arguments. For example, a function that increments an integer is given by the partial application $add' \; 1 :: Int \to Int$ of the curried function add' with only one of its two arguments.

To avoid excess parentheses when working with curried functions, two simple conventions are adopted. First of all, the function arrow $\to$ in types is assumed to associate to the right. For example,

$$Int \to Int \to Int \to Int$$

means

$$Int \to (Int \to (Int \to Int))$$

Consequently, function application, which is denoted silently using spacing, is assumed to associate to the left. For example,

$$mult \; x \; y \; z$$

means

$$((mult \; x) \; y) \; z$$

Unless tupling is explicitly required, all functions in Haskell with multiple arguments are normally defined as curried functions, and the two conventions above are used to reduce the number of parentheses that are required.

3.7 | Polymorphic types

The library function *length* calculates the length of any list, irrespective of the type of the elements of the list. For example, it can be used to calculate the length of a list of integers, a list of strings, or even a list of functions:

```
>  length [1, 3, 5, 7]
4
```

```
>  length ["Yes", "No"]
2
```

```
>  length [isDigit, isLower, isUpper]
3
```

The idea that *length* can be applied to lists whose elements have any type is made precise in its type by the inclusion of a *type variable*. Type variables must begin with a lower-case letter, and are usually simply named a, b, c, and so on. For example, the type of *length* is as follows:

$$length \ :: \ [a] \to Int$$

That is, for any type a, the function *length* has type $[a] \to Int$. A type that contains one or more type variables is called *polymorphic* ("of many forms"), as is an expression with such a type. Hence, $[a] \to Int$ is a polymorphic type and *length* is a polymorphic function. More generally, many of the functions provided in the standard prelude are polymorphic. For example:

$$
\begin{aligned}
fst \quad & :: \ (a, b) \to a \\
head \quad & :: \ [a] \to a \\
take \quad & :: \ Int \to [a] \to [a] \\
zip \quad & :: \ [a] \to [b] \to [(a, b)] \\
id \quad & :: \ a \to a
\end{aligned}
$$

3.8 | Overloaded types

The arithmetic operator $+$ calculates the sum of any two numbers of the same numeric type. For example, it can be used to calculate the sum of two integers, or the sum of two floating-point numbers:

```
>  1 + 2
3
```

```
>  1.1 + 2.2
3.3
```

The idea that $+$ can be applied to numbers of any numeric type is made precise in its type by the inclusion of a *class constraint*. Class constraints are written in the form $C\ a$, where C is the name of a class and a is a type variable. For example, the type of $+$ is as follows:

$$(+) \ :: \ Num\ a \Rightarrow a \to a \to a$$

That is, for any type a that is a *instance* of the class Num of numeric types, the function $(+)$ has type $a \to a \to a$. (Parenthesising an operator converts it into a curried function, and is explained in more detail in the next chapter.) A type that contains one or more class constraints is called *overloaded*, as is an expression with such a type. Hence, $Num\ a \Rightarrow a \to a \to a$ is an overloaded type and $(+)$ is an overloaded function. More generally, most of the numeric functions provided in the standard prelude are overloaded. For example:

$$
\begin{array}{lll}
(-) & :: & Num\ a \Rightarrow a \to a \to a \\
(*) & :: & Num\ a \Rightarrow a \to a \to a \\
negate & :: & Num\ a \Rightarrow a \to a \\
abs & :: & Num\ a \Rightarrow a \to a \\
signum & :: & Num\ a \Rightarrow a \to a \\
\end{array}
$$

Moreover, numbers themselves are also overloaded. For example, $3 :: Num\ a \Rightarrow a$ means that for any numeric type a, the number 3 has type a.

3.9 | Basic classes

Recall that a type is a collection of related values. Building upon this notion, a *class* is a collection of types that support certain overloaded operations called *methods*. Haskell provides a number of basic classes that are built-in to the language, of which the most commonly used are described below.

Eq – equality types

This class contains types whose values can be compared for equality and inequality using the following two methods:

$$
\begin{array}{lll}
(==) & :: & a \to a \to Bool \\
(\neq) & :: & a \to a \to Bool \\
\end{array}
$$

All the basic types $Bool$, $Char$, $String$, Int, $Integer$, and $Float$ are instances of the Eq class, as are list and tuple types, provided that their element and component types are instances of the class. For example:

```
> False == False
True

> 'a' == 'b'
False

> "abc" == "abc"
True
```

> $[1, 2] == [1, 2, 3]$
False

> $('a', False) == ('a', False)$
True

Note that function types are not in general instances of the *Eq* class, because it is not feasible in general to compare two functions for equality.

Ord – ordered types

This class contains types that are instances of the equality class *Eq*, but in addition whose values are totally (linearly) ordered, and as such can be compared and processed using the following six methods:

$$(<) \quad :: \quad a \rightarrow a \rightarrow Bool$$
$$(\leq) \quad :: \quad a \rightarrow a \rightarrow Bool$$
$$(>) \quad :: \quad a \rightarrow a \rightarrow Bool$$
$$(\geq) \quad :: \quad a \rightarrow a \rightarrow Bool$$
$$min \quad :: \quad a \rightarrow a \rightarrow a$$
$$max \quad :: \quad a \rightarrow a \rightarrow a$$

All the basic types *Bool*, *Char*, *String*, *Int*, *Integer*, and *Float* are instances of the *Ord* class, as are list types and tuple types, provided that their element and component types are instances of the class. For example:

> *False < True*
True

> *min 'a' 'b'*
'a'

> "elegant" < "elephant"
True

> $[1, 2, 3] < [1, 2]$
False

> $('a', 2) < ('b', 1)$
True

> $('a', 2) < ('a', 1)$
False

Note that strings, lists and tuples are ordered *lexicographically*; that is, in the same way as words in a dictionary. For example, two pairs of the same type are in order if their first components are in order, in which case their second components are not considered, or if their first components are equal, in which case their second components must be in order.

Show – showable types

This class contains types whose values can be converted into strings of characters using the following method:

> $show$ :: $a \rightarrow String$

All the basic types *Bool*, *Char*, *String*, *Int*, *Integer*, and *Float* are instances of the *Show* class, as are list types and tuple types, provided that their element and component types are instances of the class. For example:

```
> show False
"False"

> show 'a'
"'a'"

> show 123
"123"

> show [1, 2, 3]
"[1,2,3]"

> show ('a', False)
"('a',False)"
```

Read – readable types

This class is dual to *Show*, and contains types whose values can be converted from strings of characters using the following method:

> $read$ :: $String \rightarrow a$

All the basic types *Bool*, *Char*, *String*, *Int*, *Integer*, and *Float* are instances of the *Read* class, as are list types and tuple types, provided that their element and component types are instances of the class. For example:

```
> read "False" :: Bool
False

> read "'a'" :: Char
'a'

> read "123" :: Int
123

> read "[1,2,3]" :: [Int]
[1, 2, 3]

> read "('a',False)" :: (Char, Bool)
('a', False)
```

The use of :: in these examples resolves the type of the result. In practice, however, the necessary type information can usually be inferred automatically from the context. For example, the expression ¬ (*read* "False") requires no explicit type information, because the application of the logical negation function ¬ implies that *read* "False" must have type *Bool*.

Note that the result of *read* is undefined if its argument is not syntactically valid. For example, the expression ¬ (*read* "hello") produces an error when evaluated, because "hello" cannot be read as a logical value.

Num – numeric types

This class contains types that are instances of the equality class *Eq* and showable class *Show*, but in addition whose values are numeric, and as such can be processed using the following six methods:

$$
\begin{array}{lll}
(+) & :: & a \rightarrow a \rightarrow a \\
(-) & :: & a \rightarrow a \rightarrow a \\
(*) & :: & a \rightarrow a \rightarrow a \\
negate & :: & a \rightarrow a \\
abs & :: & a \rightarrow a \\
signum & :: & a \rightarrow a
\end{array}
$$

(The method *negate* returns the negation of a number, *abs* returns the absolute value, while *signum* returns the sign.) The basic types *Int*, *Integer*, and *Float* are instances of the *Num* class. For example:

```
>  1 + 2
3

>  1.1 + 2.2
3.3

>  negate 3.3
−3.3

>  abs (−3)
3

>  signum (−3)
−1
```

Note that the *Num* class does not provide a division method, but as we shall now see, division is handled separately using two special classes, one for integral numbers and one for fractional numbers.

Integral – integral types

This class contains types that are instances of the numeric class *Num*, but in addition whose values are integers, and as such support the methods of integer division and integer remainder:

$$
\begin{array}{lll}
div & :: & a \rightarrow a \rightarrow a \\
mod & :: & a \rightarrow a \rightarrow a
\end{array}
$$

In practice, these two methods are often written between their two arguments by enclosing their names in single back quotes. The basic types *Int* and *Integer* are instances of the *Integral* class. For example:

```
> 7 `div` 2
3

> 7 `mod` 2
1
```

For efficiency reasons, a number of prelude functions that involve both lists and integers (such as *length*, *take*, and *drop*) are restricted to the type *Int* of finite-precision integers, rather than being applicable to any instance of the *Integral* class. If required, however, such generic versions of these functions are provided as part of an additional library file called *List.hs*.

Fractional – fractional types

This class contains types that are instances of the numeric class *Num*, but in addition whose values are non-integral, and as such support the methods of fractional division and fractional reciprocation:

```
(/)    :: a → a → a
recip  :: a → a
```

The basic type *Float* is an instance of the *Fractional* class. For example:

```
> 7.0 / 2.0
3.5

> recip 2.0
0.5
```

3.10 | Chapter remarks

The term *Bool* for the type of logical values celebrates the pioneering work of George Boole on symbolic logic, while the term *curried* for functions that take their arguments one at a time celebrates the work of Haskell Curry (after whom the language Haskell itself is named) on such functions. A more detailed account of the type system is given in Haskell Report (25), while formal descriptions for specialists can be found in (20; 6).

3.11 | Exercises

1. What are the types of the following values?

['a', 'b', 'c']

('a', 'b', 'c')

[(*False*, '0'), (*True*, '1')]

([*False*, *True*], ['0', '1'])

[*tail*, *init*, *reverse*]

2. What are the types of the following functions?

$$
\begin{aligned}
second\ xs\ &=\ head\ (tail\ xs) \\
swap\ (x,\ y)\ &=\ (y,\ x) \\
pair\ x\ y\ &=\ (x,\ y) \\
double\ x\ &=\ x * 2 \\
palindrome\ xs\ &=\ reverse\ xs == xs \\
twice\ f\ x\ &=\ f\ (f\ x)
\end{aligned}
$$

Hint: take care to include the necessary class constraints if the functions are defined using overloaded operators.

3. Check your answers to the preceding two questions using Hugs.

4. Why is it not feasible in general for function types to be instances of the *Eq* class? When is it feasible? Hint: two functions of the same type are equal if they always return equal results for equal arguments.

chapter 4

Defining functions

In this chapter we introduce a range of mechanisms for defining functions in Haskell. We start with conditional expressions and guarded equations, then introduce the simple but powerful idea of pattern matching, and conclude with the concepts of lambda expressions and sections.

4.1 | New from old

Perhaps the most straightforward way to define new functions is simply by combining one or more existing functions. For example, a number of library functions that are defined in this way are shown below.

- Decide if a character is a digit:

$$isDigit \quad :: \quad Char \rightarrow Bool$$
$$isDigit \; c \; = \; c \geq {\,}'0' \wedge c \leq {\,}'9'$$

- Decide if an integer is even:

$$even \quad :: \quad Integral \; a \Rightarrow a \rightarrow Bool$$
$$even \; n \; = \; n \; {\text{'}mod\text{'}} \; 2 == 0$$

- Split a list at the nth element:

$$splitAt \quad :: \quad Int \rightarrow [\,a\,] \rightarrow ([\,a\,], [\,a\,])$$
$$splitAt \; n \; xs \; = \; (take \; n \; xs, \; drop \; n \; xs)$$

- Reciprocation:

$$recip \quad :: \quad Fractional \; a \Rightarrow a \rightarrow a$$
$$recip \; n \; = \; 1 \,/\, n$$

Note the use of the class constraints in the types for *even* and *recip* above, which make precise the idea that these functions can be applied to numbers of any integral and fractional types, respectively.

4.2 | Conditional expressions

Haskell provides a range of different ways to define functions that choose between a number of possible results. The simplest are *conditional expressions*, which use a logical expression called a *condition* to choose between two results of the same type. If the condition is *True*, then the first result is chosen, and if it is *False*, then the second result is chosen. For example, the library function *abs* that returns the absolute value of an integer can be defined as follows:

$$abs \quad :: \quad Int \to Int$$
$$abs\ n \quad = \quad \textbf{if}\ n \geq 0\ \textbf{then}\ n\ \textbf{else} - n$$

Conditional expressions may be nested, in the sense that they can contain other conditional expressions. For example, the library function *signum* that returns the sign of an integer can be defined as follows:

$$signum \quad :: \quad Int \to Int$$
$$signum\ n \quad = \quad \textbf{if}\ n < 0\ \textbf{then} - 1\ \textbf{else}$$
$$\textbf{if}\ n == 0\ \textbf{then}\ 0\ \textbf{else}\ 1$$

Note that unlike in some programming languages, conditional expressions in Haskell must always have an **else** branch, which avoids the well-known "dangling else" problem. For example, if **else** branches were optional, then the expression **if** *True* **then if** *False* **then** 1 **else** 2 could either return the result 2 or produce an error, depending upon whether the single **else** branch was assumed to be part of the inner or outer conditional expression.

4.3 | Guarded equations

As an alternative to using conditional expressions, functions can also be defined using *guarded equations*, in which a sequence of logical expressions called *guards* is used to choose between a sequence of results of the same type. If the first guard is *True*, then the first result is chosen; otherwise, if the second is *True*, then the second result is chosen, and so on. For example, the library function *abs* can also be defined as follows:

$$abs\ n \mid n \geq 0 \qquad = \quad n$$
$$\mid otherwise \quad = \quad -n$$

The symbol | is read as "such that", and the guard *otherwise* is defined in the standard prelude simply by *otherwise* = *True*. Ending a sequence of guards with *otherwise* is not necessary, but provides a convenient way of handling "all other cases", as well as clearly avoiding the possibility that none of the guards in the sequence is *True*, which would result in an error.

The main benefit of guarded equations over conditional expressions is that definitions with multiple guards are easier to read. For example, the library function *signum* is easier to understand when defined as follows:

$$signum\ n \mid n < 0 \quad = \quad -1$$
$$\mid n == 0 \quad = \quad 0$$
$$\mid otherwise \quad = \quad 1$$

4.4 | Pattern matching

Many functions have a particularly simple and intuitive definition using *pattern matching*, in which a sequence of syntactic expressions called *patterns* is used to choose between a sequence of results of the same type. If the first pattern is *matched*, then the first result is chosen; otherwise, if the second is matched, then the second result is chosen, and so on. For example, the library function $\neg$ that returns the negation of a logical value is defined as follows:

$$\neg \qquad :: \quad Bool \to Bool$$
$$\neg\ False \quad = \quad True$$
$$\neg\ True \quad = \quad False$$

Functions with more than one argument can also be defined using pattern matching, in which case the patterns for each argument are matched in order within each equation. For example, the library operator $\wedge$ that returns the conjunction of two logical values can be defined as follows:

$$(\wedge) \qquad :: \quad Bool \to Bool \to Bool$$
$$True \wedge True \quad = \quad True$$
$$True \wedge False \quad = \quad False$$
$$False \wedge True \quad = \quad False$$
$$False \wedge False \quad = \quad False$$

However, this definition can be simplified by combining the last three equations into a single equation that returns *False* independent of the values of the two arguments, using the *wildcard* pattern _ that matches any value:

$$True \wedge True \quad = \quad True$$
$$\_ \wedge \_ \qquad = \quad False$$

This version also has the benefit that, under lazy evaluation as discussed in chapter 12, if the first argument is *False*, then the result *False* is returned without the need to evaluate the second argument. In practice, the prelude defines $\wedge$ using equations that have this same property, but make the choice about which equation applies using the value of the first argument only:

$$True \wedge b \quad = \quad b$$
$$False \wedge \_ \quad = \quad False$$

That is, if the first argument is *True*, then the result is the value of the second argument, and, if the first argument is *False*, then the result is *False*.

Note that for technical reasons the same name may not be used for more than one argument in a single equation. For example, the following definition for the operator $\wedge$ is based upon the observation that, if the two arguments are equal, then the result is the same value, otherwise the result is *False*, but is invalid because of the above naming requirement:

$$b \wedge b = b$$
$$\_ \wedge \_ = False$$

If desired, however, a valid version of this definition can be obtained by using a guard to decide if the two arguments are equal:

$$b \wedge c \mid b == c = b$$
$$\mid otherwise = False$$

So far, we have only considered basic patterns that are either values, variables, or the wildcard pattern. In the remainder of this section we introduce three useful ways to build larger patterns by combining smaller patterns.

Tuple patterns

A tuple of patterns is itself a pattern, which matches any tuple of the same arity whose components all match the corresponding patterns in order. For example, the library functions *fst* and *snd* that select the first and second components of a pair are defined as follows:

$$fst \quad :: \quad (a, b) \to a$$
$$fst\ (x, \_) = x$$
$$snd \quad :: \quad (a, b) \to b$$
$$snd\ (\_, y) = y$$

List patterns

Similarly, a list of patterns is itself a pattern, which matches any list of the same length whose elements all match the corresponding patterns in order. For example, a function *test* that decides if a list contains precisely three characters beginning with 'a' can be defined as follows:

$$test \quad :: \quad [Char] \to Bool$$
$$test\ ['a', \_, \_] = True$$
$$test\ \_ = False$$

Up to this point we have viewed lists as a primitive notion in Haskell. In fact they are not primitive as such, but are actually constructed one element at a time starting from the empty list [] using an operator : called *cons* that *cons*tructs a new list by prepending a new element to the start of an existing list. For example, the list [1, 2, 3] can be decomposed as follows:

$$[1, 2, 3]$$
$$= \quad \{ \text{list notation} \}$$
$$1 : [2, 3]$$
$$= \quad \{ \text{list notation} \}$$
$$1 : (2 : [3])$$
$$= \quad \{ \text{list notation} \}$$
$$1 : (2 : (3 : []))$$

That is, [1, 2, 3] is just an abbreviation for $1 : (2 : (3 : []))$. To avoid excess parentheses when working with such lists, the cons operator is assumed to associate to the right. For example, $1 : 2 : 3 : []$ means $1 : (2 : (3 : []))$.

As well as being used to construct lists, the cons operator can also be used to construct patterns, which match any non-empty list whose first and remaining elements match the corresponding patterns in order. For example, we can now define a more general version of the function *test* that decides if a list containing any number of characters begins with 'a':

$$
\begin{aligned}
test &\quad :: \quad [\,Char\,] \rightarrow Bool \\
test\,(\text{'a'}:\_) &\quad = \quad True \\
test\,\_ &\quad = \quad False
\end{aligned}
$$

Similarly, the library functions *null*, *head* and *tail* that decide if a list is empty, select the first element of a non-empty list, and remove the first element of a non-empty list are defined as follows:

$$
\begin{aligned}
null &\quad :: \quad [\,a\,] \rightarrow Bool \\
null\,[\,] &\quad = \quad True \\
null\,(\_:\_) &\quad = \quad False \\[4pt]
head &\quad :: \quad [\,a\,] \rightarrow a \\
head\,(x:\_) &\quad = \quad x \\[4pt]
tail &\quad :: \quad [\,a\,] \rightarrow [\,a\,] \\
tail\,(\_:xs) &\quad = \quad xs
\end{aligned}
$$

Note that cons patterns must be parenthesised, because function application has higher priority than all other operators. For example, the definition $tail\,\_:xs = xs$ without parentheses means $(tail\,\_):xs = xs$, which is both the incorrect meaning and an invalid definition.

Integer patterns

As a special case that is sometimes useful, Haskell also allows integer patterns of the form $n + k$, where n is an integer variable and $k > 0$ is an integer constant. For example, a function *pred* that maps zero to itself and any strictly positive integer to its predecessor can be defined as follows:

$$
\begin{aligned}
pred &\quad :: \quad Int \rightarrow Int \\
pred\,0 &\quad = \quad 0 \\
pred\,(n+1) &\quad = \quad n
\end{aligned}
$$

There are two points to note about $n + k$ patterns. First of all, they only match integers $\geq k$. For example, evaluating $pred\,(-1)$ produces an error, because neither of the two patterns in the definition for *pred* matches negative integers. Secondly, for the same reason as cons patterns, integer patterns must be parenthesised. For example, the definition $pred\,n + 1 = n$ without parentheses means $(pred\,n) + 1 = n$, which is an invalid definition.

4.5 | Lambda expressions

As an alternative to defining functions using equations, functions can also be constructed using *lambda expressions*, which comprise a pattern for each of the arguments, a body that specifies how the result can be calculated in terms of the arguments, but do not give a name for the function itself. In other words, lambda expressions are nameless functions.

For example, a nameless function that takes a single number x as its argument, and produces the result $x + x$, can be constructed as follows:

$$\lambda x \rightarrow x + x$$

The symbol λ is the lower-case Greek letter "lambda". Despite the fact that they have no names, functions constructed using lambda expressions can be used in the same way as any other functions. For example:

```
>  (λx → x + x) 2
4
```

As well as being interesting in their own right, lambda expressions have a number of practical applications. First of all, they can be used to formalise the meaning of curried function definitions. For example, the definition

$$add \ x \ y \ = \ x + y$$

can be understood as meaning

$$add \ = \ \lambda x \rightarrow (\lambda y \rightarrow x + y)$$

which makes precise that add is a function that takes a number x and returns a function, which in turn takes a number y and returns the result $x + y$.

Secondly, lambda expressions are also useful when defining functions that return functions as results by their very nature, rather than as a consequence of currying. For example, the library function $const$ that returns a constant function that always produces a given value can be defined as follows:

```
const     ::  a → b → a
const x _ =  x
```

However, it is more appealing to define $const$ in a way that makes explicit that it returns a function as its result, by including parentheses in the type and using a lambda expression in the definition itself:

```
const   ::  a → (b → a)
const x =  λ_ → x
```

Finally, lambda expressions can be used to avoid having to name a function that is only referenced once. For example, a function $odds$ that returns the first n odd integers can be defined as follows:

```
odds    ::  Int → [Int]
odds n  =  map f [0..n − 1]
               where f x = x * 2 + 1
```

(The library function map applies a function to all elements of a list.) However, because the locally defined function f is only referenced once, the definition for $odds$ can be simplified by using a lambda expression:

```
odds n  =  map (λx → x * 2 + 1) [0..n − 1]
```

4.6 | Sections

Functions such as $+$ that are written between their two arguments are called *operators*. As we have already seen, any function with two arguments can be converted into an operator by enclosing the name of the function in single back quotes, as in 7 `div` 2. However, the converse is also possible. In particular, any operator can be converted into a curried function that is written before its arguments by enclosing the name of the operator in parentheses, as in $(+)$ 1 2. Moreover, this convention also allows one of the arguments to be included in the parentheses if desired, as in $(1+)$ 2 and $(+2)$ 1.

In general, if $\oplus$ is an operator, then expressions of the form $(\oplus)$, $(x \oplus)$, and $(\oplus\ y)$ for arguments x and y are called *sections*, whose meaning as functions can be formalised using lambda expressions as follows:

$$
\begin{aligned}
(\oplus) &= \lambda x \to (\lambda y \to x \oplus y) \\
(x \oplus) &= \lambda y \to x \oplus y \\
(\oplus\ y) &= \lambda x \to x \oplus y
\end{aligned}
$$

Sections have three main applications. First of all, they can be used to construct a number of simple but useful functions in a particularly compact way, as shown in the following examples:

$(+)$ is the addition function $\lambda x \to (\lambda y \to x + y)$

$(1+)$ is the successor function $\lambda y \to 1 + y$

$(1/)$ is the reciprocation function $\lambda y \to 1\ /\ y$

$(*2)$ is the doubling function $\lambda x \to x * 2$

$(/2)$ is the halving function $\lambda x \to x\ /\ 2$

Secondly, sections are necessary when stating the type of operators, because an operator itself is not a valid expression in Haskell. For example, the type of the logical conjunction operator $\wedge$ is stated as follows:

$$(\wedge)\ ::\quad Bool \to Bool \to Bool$$

Finally, sections are also necessary when using operators as arguments to other functions. For example, the library function *and* that decides if all logical values in a list are *True* is defined by using the operator $\wedge$ as an argument to the library function *foldr*, which is itself discussed in chapter 7:

$$
\begin{aligned}
and\ &::\quad [Bool] \to Bool \\
and\ &=\quad foldr\ (\wedge)\ True
\end{aligned}
$$

4.7 | Chapter remarks

A formal meaning for pattern matching by translation using more primitive features of the language is given in the Haskell Report (25). The Greek letter λ used when defining nameless functions comes from the *lambda calculus*, the mathematical theory of functions upon which Haskell is founded.

4.8 | Exercises

1. Using library functions, define a function *halve* :: [a] → ([a], [a]) that splits an even-lengthed list into two halves. For example:

    > *halve* [1, 2, 3, 4, 5, 6]
    ([1, 2, 3], [4, 5, 6])

2. Consider a function *safetail* :: [a] → [a] that behaves as the library function *tail*, except that *safetail* maps the empty list to itself, whereas *tail* produces an error in this case. Define *safetail* using:

    (a) a conditional expression;
    (b) guarded equations;
    (c) pattern matching.

    Hint: make use of the library function *null*.

3. In a similar way to ∧, show how the logical disjunction operator ∨ can be defined in four different ways using pattern matching.

4. Redefine the following version of the conjunction operator using conditional expressions rather than pattern matching:

    True ∧ *True*   =   *True*
    _ ∧ _   =   *False*

5. Do the same for the following version, and note the difference in the number of conditional expressions required:

    True ∧ *b* = *b*
    False ∧ _ = *False*

6. Show how the curried function definition *mult x y z = x * y * z* can be understood in terms of lambda expressions.

chapter 5

List comprehensions

In this chapter we introduce list comprehensions, which allow many functions on lists to be defined in simple manner. We start by explaining generators and guards, then introduce the function *zip* and the idea of string comprehensions, and conclude by developing a program to crack the Caesar cipher.

5.1 | Generators

In mathematics, the *comprehension* notation can be used to construct new sets from existing sets. For example, the comprehension $\{x^2 \mid x \in \{1 \ldots 5\}\}$ produces the set $\{1, 4, 9, 16, 25\}$ of all numbers x^2 such that x is an element of the set $\{1 \ldots 5\}$. In Haskell, a similar comprehension notation can be used to construct new lists from existing lists. For example:

```
> [x ↑ 2 | x ← [1..5]]
[1, 4, 9, 16, 25]
```

The symbols | and ← are read as "such that" and "is drawn from" respectively, and the expression $x \leftarrow [1 \ldots 5]$ is called a *generator*. A list comprehension can have more than one generator, with successive generators being separated by commas. For example, the list of all possible pairings of an element from the list $[1, 2, 3]$ with an element from $[4, 5]$ can be produced as follows:

```
> [(x, y) | x ← [1, 2, 3], y ← [4, 5]]
[(1, 4), (1, 5), (2, 4), (2, 5), (3, 4), (3, 5)]
```

Changing the order of the two generators in this example produces the same set of pairs, but arranged in a different order:

```
> [(x, y) | y ← [4, 5], x ← [1, 2, 3]]
[(1, 4), (2, 4), (3, 4), (1, 5), (2, 5), (3, 5)]
```

In particular, whereas in this case the x components of the pairs change more frequently than the y components (1,2,3,1,2,3 versus 4,4,4,5,5,5), in the previous case the y components change more frequently than the x components

(4,5,4,5,4,5 versus 1,1,2,2,3,3). These behaviours can be understood by thinking of later generators as being more deeply nested, and hence changing the values of their variables more frequently than earlier generators.

Later generators can also depend upon the values of variables from earlier generators. For example, the list of all possible ordered pairings of elements from the list $[1 .. 3]$ can be produced as follows:

> $[(x, y) \mid x \leftarrow [1 .. 3], y \leftarrow [x .. 3]]$
> $[(1, 1), (1, 2), (1, 3), (2, 2), (2, 3), (3, 3)]$

As another example of this idea, the library function *concat* that concatenates a list of lists can be defined by using one generator to select each list in turn, and another to select each element from each list:

$concat \quad :: \quad [[a]] \rightarrow [a]$
$concat\ xss \quad = \quad [x \mid xs \leftarrow xss, x \leftarrow xs]$

The wildcard pattern _ is sometimes useful in generators to discard certain elements from a list. For example, a function that selects all the first components from a list of pairs can be defined as follows:

$firsts \quad :: \quad [(a, b)] \rightarrow [a]$
$firsts\ ps \quad = \quad [x \mid (x, \_) \leftarrow ps]$

Similarly, the library function that calculates the *length* of a list can be defined by replacing each element by one and summing the resulting list:

$length \quad :: \quad [a] \rightarrow Int$
$length\ xs \quad = \quad sum\ [1 \mid \_ \leftarrow xs]$

In this case, the generator $\_ \leftarrow xs$ simply serves as a counter to govern the production of the appropriate number of ones.

5.2 | Guards

List comprehensions can also use logical expressions called *guards* to filter the values produced by earlier generators. If a guard is *True*, then the current values are retained, and, if it is *False*, then they are discarded. For example, the comprehension $[x \mid x \leftarrow [1 .. 10], even\ x]$ produces the list $[2, 4, 6, 8, 10]$ of all even numbers from the list $[1 .. 10]$. Similarly, a function that maps a positive integer to its list of positive *factors* can be defined as follows:

$factors \quad :: \quad Int \rightarrow [Int]$
$factors\ n \quad = \quad [x \mid x \leftarrow [1 .. n], n\ `mod`\ x == 0]$

For example:

> $factors\ 15$
> $[1, 3, 5, 15]$

> $factors\ 7$
> $[1, 7]$

Recall that an integer greater than one is *prime* if its only positive factors are one and the number itself. Hence, by using *factors*, a simple function that decides if an integer is prime can be defined as follows:

$$
\begin{aligned}
prime &:: & & Int \to Bool \\
prime\ n &= & & factors\ n == [1, n]
\end{aligned}
$$

For example:

```
> prime 15
False

> prime 7
True
```

Note that deciding that a number such as 15 is not prime does not require the function *prime* to produce all of its factors, because under lazy evaluation the result *False* is returned as soon as any factor other than one or the number itself is produced, which for this example is given by the factor 3.

Returning to list comprehensions, using *prime* we can now define a function that produces the list of all prime numbers up to a given limit:

$$
\begin{aligned}
primes &:: & & Int \to [Int] \\
primes\ n &= & & [x \mid x \leftarrow [2 .. n], prime\ x]
\end{aligned}
$$

For example:

```
> primes 40
[2, 3, 5, 7, 11, 13, 17, 19, 23, 29, 31, 37]
```

In chapter 12 we will present a more efficient program to generate prime numbers using the famous "sieve of Eratosthenes", which has a particularly clear and concise implementation in Haskell.

As a final example concerning guards, suppose that we represent a lookup table by a list of pairs comprising keys and values. Then for any type of keys that is an equality type, a function *find* that returns the list of all values that are associated with a given key in a table can be defined as follows:

$$
\begin{aligned}
find &:: & & Eq\ a \Rightarrow a \to [(a, b)] \to [b] \\
find\ k\ t &= & & [v \mid (k', v) \leftarrow t, k == k']
\end{aligned}
$$

For example:

```
> find 'b' [('a', 1), ('b', 2), ('c', 3), ('b', 4)]
[2, 4]
```

5.3 | The *zip* function

The library function *zip* produces a new list by pairing successive elements from two existing lists until either or both are exhausted. For example:

```
> zip ['a', 'b', 'c'] [1, 2, 3, 4]
[('a', 1), ('b', 2), ('c', 3)]
```

The function *zip* is often useful when programming with list comprehensions. For example, suppose that we define a function *pairs* that returns the list of all pairs of adjacent elements from a list as follows:

$$
\begin{array}{lll}
pairs & :: & [a] \to [(a, a)] \\
pairs\ xs & = & zip\ xs\ (tail\ xs)
\end{array}
$$

For example:

> *pairs* $[1, 2, 3, 4]$
$[(1, 2), (2, 3), (3, 4)]$

Then using *pairs* we can now define a function that decides if a list of elements of any ordered type is *sorted* by simply checking that all pairs of adjacent elements from the list are in the correct order:

$$
\begin{array}{lll}
sorted & :: & Ord\ a \Rightarrow [a] \to Bool \\
sorted\ xs & = & and\ [x \leq y \mid (x, y) \leftarrow pairs\ xs]
\end{array}
$$

For example:

> *sorted* $[1, 2, 3, 4]$
True

> *sorted* $[1, 3, 2, 4]$
False

Similarly to the function *prime*, deciding that a list such as $[1, 3, 2, 4]$ is not sorted may not require the function *sorted* to produce all pairs of adjacent elements, because the result *False* is returned as soon as any non-ordered pair is produced, which in this example is given by the pair $(3, 2)$.

Using *zip* we can also define a function that returns the list of all *positions* at which a value occurs in a list, by pairing each element with its position, and selecting those positions at which the desired value occurs:

$$
\begin{array}{lll}
positions & :: & Eq\ a \Rightarrow a \to [a] \to [Int] \\
positions\ x\ xs & = & [i \mid (x', i) \leftarrow zip\ xs\ [0 .. n], x == x'] \\
& & \textbf{where}\ n = length\ xs - 1
\end{array}
$$

For example:

> *positions* False $[$ *True*, *False*, *True*, *False* $]$
$[1, 3]$

5.4 | String comprehensions

Up to this point we have viewed strings as a primitive notion in Haskell. In fact they are not primitive as such, but are actually constructed as lists of characters. For example, "abc" :: *String* is just an abbreviation for $['a', 'b', 'c'] ::$

[*Char*]. Because strings are just special kinds of lists, any polymorphic function on lists can also be used with strings. For example:

```
> "abcde" !! 2
'c'

> take 3 "abcde"
"abc"

> length "abcde"
5

> zip "abc" [1, 2, 3, 4]
[('a', 1), ('b', 2), ('c', 3)]
```

For the same reason, list comprehensions can also be used to define functions on strings, such as functions that return the number of lower-case letters and particular characters that occur in a string, respectively:

$$
\begin{array}{lll}
lowers & :: & String \rightarrow Int \\
lowers\ xs & = & length\ [x \mid x \leftarrow xs, isLower\ x] \\
count & :: & Char \rightarrow String \rightarrow Int \\
count\ x\ xs & = & length\ [x' \mid x' \leftarrow xs, x == x']
\end{array}
$$

For example:

```
> lowers "Haskell"
6

> count 's' "Mississippi"
4
```

5.5 | The Caesar cipher

We conclude this chapter with an extended example. Consider the problem of encoding a string in order to disguise its contents from unintended readers. A well-known encoding method is the *Caesar cipher*, named after its use by Julius Caesar. To encode a string, Caesar simply replaced each letter in the string by the letter three places further down in the alphabet, wrapping around at the end of the alphabet. For example, the string

```
"haskell is fun"
```

would be encoded as

```
"kdvnhoo lv ixq"
```

More generally, the shift factor of three used by Caesar can be replaced by any integer between one and twenty-five, thereby giving twenty-five different ways of encoding a string. For example, with a shift factor of ten, the original string above would be encoded as

```
"rkcuovv sc pex"
```

In the remainder of this section we show how Haskell can be used to implement the Caesar cipher, and how the cipher itself can easily be "cracked" by exploiting information about letter frequencies.

Encoding and decoding

For simplicity, we will only encode the lower-case letters within a string, leaving other characters such as upper-case letters and punctuation unchanged. We begin by defining a function *let2int* that converts a lower-case letter between 'a' and 'z' into the corresponding integer between 0 and 25, together with a function *int2let* that performs the opposite conversion:

$$
\begin{aligned}
&let2int &&::&& Char \to Int \\
&let2int\ c &&=&& ord\ c - ord\ 'a' \\
\\
&int2let &&::&& Int \to Char \\
&int2let\ n &&=&& chr\ (ord\ 'a' + n)
\end{aligned}
$$

(The library functions $ord :: Char \to Int$ and $chr :: Int \to Char$ convert between characters and their Unicode representation as integers.) For example:

```
> let2int 'a'
0

> int2let 0
'a'
```

Using these two functions, we can define a function *shift* that applies a shift factor to a lower-case letter by converting the letter into the corresponding integer, adding on the shift factor and taking the remainder when divided by twenty-six (thereby wrapping around at the end of the alphabet), and converting the resulting integer back into a lower-case letter:

$$
\begin{aligned}
&shift &&::&& Int \to Char \to Char \\
&shift\ n\ c\ |\ isLower\ c &&=&& int2let\ ((let2int\ c + n)\ `mod`\ 26) \\
&\quad\quad\ |\ otherwise &&=&& c
\end{aligned}
$$

Note that this function accepts both positive and negative shift factors, and that only lower-case letters are changed. For example:

```
> shift 3 'a'
'd'

> shift 3 'z'
'c'

> shift (−3) 'c'
'z'

> shift 3 ' '
' '
```

Using *shift* within a string comprehension, it is now easy to define a function that encodes a string using a given shift factor:

$$
\begin{aligned}
encode &\; :: \; Int \to String \to String \\
encode\ n\ xs &\; = \; [shift\ n\ x \mid x \leftarrow xs]
\end{aligned}
$$

A separate function to decode a string is not required, because this can be achieved by simply using a negative shift factor. For example:

```
> encode 3 "haskell is fun"
"kdvnhoo lv ixq"

> encode (−3) "kdvnhoo lv ixq"
"haskell is fun"
```

Frequency tables

The key to cracking the Caesar cipher is the observation that some letters are used more frequently than others in English text. By analysing a large volume of text, one can derive the following table of approximate percentage frequencies of the twenty-six letters of alphabet:

$$
\begin{aligned}
table &\; :: \; [Float] \\
table &\; = \; [8.2, 1.5, 2.8, 4.3, 12.7, 2.2, 2.0, 6.1, 7.0, 0.2, 0.8, 4.0, 2.4, \\
& \qquad \quad 6.7, 7.5, 1.9, 0.1, 6.0, 6.3, 9.1, 2.8, 1.0, 2.4, 0.2, 2.0, 0.1]
\end{aligned}
$$

For example, the letter 'e' occurs most often, with a frequency of 12.7%, while 'q' and 'z' occur least often, with a frequency of just 0.1%. It is also useful to produce frequency tables for individual strings. To this end, we first define a function that calculates the percentage of one integer with respect to another, returning the result as a floating-point number:

$$
\begin{aligned}
percent &\; :: \; Int \to Int \to Float \\
percent\ n\ m &\; = \; (fromIntegral\ n\ /\ fromIntegral\ m) * 100
\end{aligned}
$$

(The library function *fromIntegral* :: $Int \to Float$ converts an integer into the corresponding floating-point number.) Using *percent* within a string comprehension, together with the functions *lowers* and *count* from the previous section, we can define a function that returns a frequency table for any string:

$$
\begin{aligned}
freqs &\; :: \; String \to [Float] \\
freqs\ xs &\; = \; [percent\ (count\ x\ xs)\ n \mid x \leftarrow ['a' \mathrel{..} 'z']] \\
& \qquad \textbf{where}\ n = lowers\ xs
\end{aligned}
$$

For example:

```
> freqs "abbcccddddeeeee"
[6.7, 13.3, 20.0, 26.7, 33.3, 0.0, 0.0, 0.0, 0.0, 0.0, 0.0, 0.0, ⋯ , 0.0]
```

That is, the letter 'a' occurs with a frequency of 6.7%, the letter 'b' with a frequency of 13.3%, and so on. The use of the local definition $n = lowers\ xs$ within *freqs* ensures that the number of lower-case letters in the argument string is calculated once, rather than each of the twenty-six times that this number is used within the string comprehension.

Cracking the cipher

A standard method for comparing a list of observed frequencies os with a list of expected frequencies es is the *chi-square* statistic, defined by the following summation in which n denotes the length of the two lists, and xs_i denotes the ith element of a list xs counting from zero:

$$\sum_{i=0}^{n-1} \frac{(os_i - es_i)^2}{es_i}$$

The details of the chi-square statistic need not concern us here, only the fact that the smaller the value it produces the better the match between the two frequency lists. Using the library function *zip* and a list comprehension, it is easy to translate the above formula into a function definition:

$$
\begin{aligned}
&chisqr & &:: & &[\,Float\,] \rightarrow [\,Float\,] \rightarrow Float \\
&chisqr\ os\ es & &= & &sum\ [((o - e) \uparrow 2)\,/\,e \mid (o,\,e) \leftarrow zip\ os\ es\,]
\end{aligned}
$$

In turn, we define a function that rotates the elements of a list n places to the left, wrapping around at the start of the list, and assuming that n is between zero and the length of the list:

$$
\begin{aligned}
&rotate & &:: & &Int \rightarrow [\,a\,] \rightarrow [\,a\,] \\
&rotate\ n\ xs & &= & &drop\ n\ xs + \!\!+ take\ n\ xs
\end{aligned}
$$

For example:

```
>  rotate 3 [1, 2, 3, 4, 5]
[4, 5, 1, 2, 3]
```

Now suppose that we are given an encoded string, but not the shift factor that was used to encode it, and wish to determine this number in order that we can decode the string. This can usually be achieved by producing the frequency table of the encoded string, calculating the chi-square statistic for each possible rotation of this table with respect to the table of expected frequencies, and using the position of the minimum chi-square value as the shift factor. For example, if $table' = freqs$ "kdvnhoo lv ixq", then

$$[\,chisqr\ (rotate\ n\ table')\ table \mid n \leftarrow [0 \,.\,.\, 25]\,]$$

gives the result

$$[\,1408.8, 640.3, 612.4, 202.6, 1439.8, 4247.2, 651.3, \cdots, 626.7\,]$$

in which the minimum value, 202.6, appears at position three in this list. Hence, we conclude that three is the most likely shift factor that was used to encode the string. Using the function *positions* from earlier in this chapter, this procedure can be implemented as follows:

$$
\begin{aligned}
&crack & &:: & &String \rightarrow String \\
&crack\ xs & &= & &encode\ (-factor)\ xs \\
&\quad\textbf{where} \\
&\qquad factor = head\ (positions\ (minimum\ chitab)\ chitab) \\
&\qquad chitab = [\,chisqr\ (rotate\ n\ table')\ table \mid n \leftarrow [0 \,.\,.\, 25]\,] \\
&\qquad table' = freqs\ xs
\end{aligned}
$$

For example:

```
> crack "kdvnhoo lv ixq"
"haskell is fun"

> crack "vscd mywzboroxcsyxc kbo ecopev"
"list comprehensions are useful"
```

More generally, the *crack* function can decode most strings produced using the Caesar cipher. Note, however, that it may not be successful if the string is short or has an unusual distribution of letters. For example:

```
> crack (encode 3 "haskell")
"piasmtt"

> crack (encode 3 "boxing wizards jump quickly")
"wjsdib rduvmyn ephk lpdxfgt"
```

5.6 | Chapter remarks

The term *comprehension* comes from the "axiom of comprehension" in set theory, which makes precise the idea of constructing a set by selecting all values satisfying a particular property. A formal meaning for list comprehensions by translation using more primitive features of the language is given in the Haskell Report (25). A popular account of the Caesar cipher, and many other famous cryptographic methods, is given in *The Code Book* (29).

5.7 | Exercises

1. Using a list comprehension, give an expression that calculates the sum $1^2 + 2^2 + \ldots 100^2$ of the first one hundred integer squares.

2. In a similar way to the function *length*, show how the library function *replicate* :: $Int \to a \to [a]$ that produces a list of identical elements can be defined using a list comprehension. For example:

```
> replicate 3 True
[True, True, True]
```

3. A triple (x, y, z) of positive integers is *pythagorean* if $x^2 + y^2 = z^2$. Using a list comprehension, define a function *pyths* :: $Int \to [(Int, Int, Int)]$ that returns the list of all pythagorean triples whose components are at most a given limit. For example:

```
> pyths 10
[(3, 4, 5), (4, 3, 5), (6, 8, 10), (8, 6, 10)]
```

4. A positive integer is *perfect* if it equals the sum of its factors, excluding the number itself. Using a list comprehension and the function *factors*, define a

function *perfects* :: *Int* → [*Int*] that returns the list of all perfect numbers up to a given limit. For example:

> *perfects* 500
[6, 28, 496]

5. Show how the single comprehension [(x, y) | x ← [1, 2, 3], y ← [4, 5, 6]] with two generators can be re-expressed using two comprehensions with single generators. Hint: make use of the library function *concat* and nest one comprehension within the other.

6. Redefine the function *positions* using the function *find*.

7. The *scalar product* of two lists of integers *xs* and *ys* of length *n* is given by the sum of the products of corresponding integers:

$$\sum_{i=0}^{n-1}(xs_i * ys_i)$$

In a similar manner to the function *chisqr*, show how a list comprehension can be used to define a function *scalarproduct* :: [*Int*] → [*Int*] → *Int* that returns the scalar product of two lists. For example:

> *scalarproduct* [1, 2, 3] [4, 5, 6]
32

8. Modify the Caesar cipher program to also handle upper-case letters.

chapter 6

Recursive functions

In this chapter we introduce recursion, the basic mechanism for looping in Haskell. We start with recursion on integers, then extend the idea to recursion on lists, consider multiple arguments, multiple recursion, and mutual recursion, and conclude with some advice on defining recursive functions.

6.1 | Basic concepts

As we have seen in previous chapters, many functions can naturally be defined in terms of other functions. For example, a function that returns the *factorial* of a non-negative integer can be defined by using library functions to calculate the product of the integers between one and the number itself:

$$
\begin{aligned}
&factorial &&::\quad Int \rightarrow Int \\
&factorial\ n &&=\quad product\ [1 .. n]
\end{aligned}
$$

In Haskell, it is also permissible to define functions in terms of themselves, in which case the functions are called *recursive*. For example, the *factorial* function can be defined in this manner as follows:

$$
\begin{aligned}
&factorial\ 0 &&=\quad 1 \\
&factorial\ (n+1) &&=\quad (n+1) * factorial\ n
\end{aligned}
$$

The first equation states that the factorial of zero is one, and is called a *base case*. The second equation states that the factorial of any strictly positive integer is the product of that number and the factorial of its predecessor, and is called a *recursive case*. For example, the following calculation shows how the factorial of three is computed using this definition:

$$
\begin{aligned}
&\quad factorial\ 3 \\
&=\quad \{ \text{applying } factorial \} \\
&\quad 3 * factorial\ 2 \\
&=\quad \{ \text{applying } factorial \} \\
&\quad 3 * (2 * factorial\ 1) \\
&=\quad \{ \text{applying } factorial \}
\end{aligned}
$$

$$3 * (2 * (1 * factorial\ 0))$$
$$=\quad \{ \text{applying } factorial \}$$
$$3 * (2 * (1 * 1))$$
$$=\quad \{ \text{applying } * \}$$
$$6$$

Note that even though the *factorial* function is defined in terms of itself, it does not loop forever. In particular, each application of *factorial* reduces the integer argument by one, until it eventually reaches zero at which point the recursion stops and the multiplications are performed. Returning one as the factorial of zero is appropriate because one is the identity for multiplication. That is, $1 * x = x$ and $x * 1 = x$ for any integer x.

For the case of the *factorial* function, the original definition using library functions is simpler than the definition using recursion. However, as we shall see in the remainder of this book, many functions have a simple and natural definition using recursion. For example, many of the library functions in Haskell are defined in this way. Moreover, as we shall see in chapter 13, defining functions using recursion also allows properties of those functions to be proved using the powerful technique of induction.

As another example of recursion on integers, consider the multiplication operator $*$ used above. For efficiency reasons, this operator is provided as a primitive in Haskell. However, for non-negative integers it can also be defined using recursion on either of its two arguments, such as the second:

$$(*) \quad\quad :: \quad Int \rightarrow Int \rightarrow Int$$
$$m * 0 \quad\quad = \quad 0$$
$$m * (n + 1) \quad = \quad m + (m * n)$$

For example:

$$4 * 3$$
$$=\quad \{ \text{applying } * \}$$
$$4 + (4 * 2)$$
$$=\quad \{ \text{applying } * \}$$
$$4 + (4 + (4 * 1))$$
$$=\quad \{ \text{applying } * \}$$
$$4 + (4 + (4 + (4 * 0)))$$
$$=\quad \{ \text{applying } * \}$$
$$4 + (4 + (4 + 0))$$
$$=\quad \{ \text{applying } + \}$$
$$12$$

That is, the recursive definition for the $*$ operator formalises the idea that multiplication can be reduced to repeated addition.

6.2 | Recursion on lists

Recursion is not restricted to functions on integers, but can also be used to define functions on lists. For example, the library function *product* used in the preceding section can be defined as follows:

$$
\begin{array}{lll}
product & :: & Num\ a \Rightarrow [\,a\,] \rightarrow a \\
product\ [\,] & = & 1 \\
product\ (n : ns) & = & n * product\ ns
\end{array}
$$

The first equation states that the product of the empty list is one, which is appropriate because one is the identity for multiplication. The second equation states that the product of any non-empty list is given by multiplying the first number and the product of the remaining list of numbers. For example:

$$
\begin{array}{ll}
& product\ [2, 3, 4] \\
= & \quad \{\ applying\ product\ \} \\
& 2 * product\ [3, 4] \\
= & \quad \{\ applying\ product\ \} \\
& 2 * (3 * product\ [4]) \\
= & \quad \{\ applying\ product\ \} \\
& 2 * (3 * (4 * product\ [\,])) \\
= & \quad \{\ applying\ product\ \} \\
& 2 * (3 * (4 * 1)) \\
= & \quad \{\ applying\ *\ \} \\
& 24
\end{array}
$$

Recall that lists in Haskell are actually constructed one element at a time using the cons operator. Hence, $[2, 3, 4]$ is just an abbreviation for $2 : (3 : (4 : [\,]))$. As another simple example of recursion on lists, the library function *length* can be defined using the same pattern of recursion as *product*:

$$
\begin{array}{lll}
length & :: & [\,a\,] \rightarrow Int \\
length\ [\,] & = & 0 \\
length\ (\_ : xs) & = & 1 + length\ xs
\end{array}
$$

That is, the length of the empty list is zero, and the length of any non-empty list is the successor of the length of its tail. Note the use of the wildcard pattern _ in the recursive case, which reflects the fact that the length of a list does not depend upon the value of its elements.

Now let us consider the library function that reverses a list. This function can be defined using recursion as follows:

$$
\begin{array}{lll}
reverse & :: & [\,a\,] \rightarrow [\,a\,] \\
reverse\ [\,] & = & [\,] \\
reverse\ (x : xs) & = & reverse\ xs \mathbin{+\!\!+} [\,x\,]
\end{array}
$$

That is, the reverse of the empty list is simply the empty list, and the reverse of any non-empty list is given by appending the reverse of its tail to a singleton list comprising the head of the list. For example:

$$
\begin{array}{ll}
& reverse\ [1, 2, 3] \\
= & \quad \{\ applying\ reverse\ \} \\
& reverse\ [2, 3] \mathbin{+\!\!+} [1] \\
= & \quad \{\ applying\ reverse\ \} \\
& (reverse\ [3] \mathbin{+\!\!+} [2]) \mathbin{+\!\!+} [1] \\
= & \quad \{\ applying\ reverse\ \} \\
& ((reverse\ [\,] \mathbin{+\!\!+} [3]) \mathbin{+\!\!+} [2]) \mathbin{+\!\!+} [1]
\end{array}
$$

$$= \quad \{ \text{applying } reverse \}$$
$$(([\,] \mathbin{+\!\!+} [3]) \mathbin{+\!\!+} [2]) \mathbin{+\!\!+} [1]$$
$$= \quad \{ \text{applying } \mathbin{+\!\!+} \}$$
$$[3, 2, 1]$$

In turn, the append operator $\mathbin{+\!\!+}$ used in the above definition of $reverse$ can itself be defined using recursion on its first argument:

$$
\begin{array}{lll}
(\mathbin{+\!\!+}) & :: & [a] \to [a] \to [a] \\
[\,] \mathbin{+\!\!+} ys & = & ys \\
(x : xs) \mathbin{+\!\!+} ys & = & x : (xs \mathbin{+\!\!+} ys)
\end{array}
$$

For example:

$$[1, 2, 3] \mathbin{+\!\!+} [4, 5]$$
$$= \quad \{ \text{applying } \mathbin{+\!\!+} \}$$
$$1 : ([2, 3] \mathbin{+\!\!+} [4, 5])$$
$$= \quad \{ \text{applying } \mathbin{+\!\!+} \}$$
$$1 : (2 : ([3] \mathbin{+\!\!+} [4, 5]))$$
$$= \quad \{ \text{applying } \mathbin{+\!\!+} \}$$
$$1 : (2 : (3 : ([\,] \mathbin{+\!\!+} [4, 5])))$$
$$= \quad \{ \text{applying } \mathbin{+\!\!+} \}$$
$$1 : (2 : (3 : [4, 5]))$$
$$= \quad \{ \text{list notation} \}$$
$$[1, 2, 3, 4, 5]$$

That is, the recursive definition for $\mathbin{+\!\!+}$ formalises the idea that two lists can be appended by copying elements from the first list until it is exhausted, at which point the second list is joined on at the end.

We conclude this section with two examples of recursion on sorted lists. First of all, a function that inserts a new element of any ordered type into a sorted list to give another sorted list can be defined as follows:

$$
\begin{array}{lll}
insert & :: & Ord\ a \Rightarrow a \to [a] \to [a] \\
insert\ x\ [\,] & = & [x] \\
insert\ x\ (y : ys)\ |\ x \le y & = & x : y : ys \\
\quad |\ otherwise & = & y : insert\ x\ ys
\end{array}
$$

That is, inserting a new element into the empty list gives a singleton list, while for a non-empty list the result depends upon the ordering of the new element x and the head of the list y. In particular, if $x \le y$, then the new element x is simply prepended to the start of the list, otherwise the head y becomes the first element of the resulting list, and we then proceed to insert the new element into the tail of the given list. For example:

$$insert\ 3\ [1, 2, 4, 5]$$
$$= \quad \{ \text{applying } insert \}$$
$$1 : insert\ 3\ [2, 4, 5]$$
$$= \quad \{ \text{applying } insert \}$$
$$1 : 2 : insert\ 3\ [4, 5]$$
$$= \quad \{ \text{applying } insert \}$$
$$1 : 2 : 3 : [4, 5]$$

$$= \quad \{ \text{ list notation } \}$$
$$[1, 2, 3, 4, 5]$$

Using *insert* we can now define a function that implements *insertion sort*, in which the empty list is already sorted, and any non-empty list is sorted by inserting its head into the list that results from sorting its tail:

$$
\begin{array}{lll}
isort & :: & Ord\ a \Rightarrow [\,a\,] \rightarrow [\,a\,] \\
isort\ [\,] & = & [\,] \\
isort\ (x : xs) & = & insert\ x\ (isort\ xs)
\end{array}
$$

For example:

$$
\begin{array}{ll}
& isort\ [3, 2, 1, 4] \\
= & \quad \{ \text{ applying } isort \} \\
& insert\ 3\ (insert\ 2\ (insert\ 1\ (insert\ 4\ [\,]))) \\
= & \quad \{ \text{ applying } insert \} \\
& insert\ 3\ (insert\ 2\ (insert\ 1\ [4])) \\
= & \quad \{ \text{ applying } insert \} \\
& insert\ 3\ (insert\ 2\ [1, 4]) \\
= & \quad \{ \text{ applying } insert \} \\
& insert\ 3\ [1, 2, 4] \\
= & \quad \{ \text{ applying } insert \} \\
& [1, 2, 3, 4]
\end{array}
$$

6.3 | Multiple arguments

Functions with multiple arguments can also be defined using recursion on more than one argument at the same time. For example, the library function *zip* that takes two lists and produces a list of pairs is defined as follows:

$$
\begin{array}{lll}
zip & :: & [\,a\,] \rightarrow [\,b\,] \rightarrow [(a, b)] \\
zip\ [\,]\ \_ & = & [\,] \\
zip\ \_\ [\,] & = & [\,] \\
zip\ (x : xs)\ (y : ys) & = & (x, y) : zip\ xs\ ys
\end{array}
$$

For example:

$$
\begin{array}{ll}
& zip\ ['a', 'b', 'c']\ [1, 2, 3, 4] \\
= & \quad \{ \text{ applying } zip \} \\
& ('a', 1) : zip\ ['b', 'c']\ [2, 3, 4] \\
= & \quad \{ \text{ applying } zip \} \\
& ('a', 1) : ('b', 2) : zip\ ['c']\ [3, 4] \\
= & \quad \{ \text{ applying } zip \} \\
& ('a', 1) : ('b', 2) : ('c', 3) : zip\ [\,]\ [4] \\
= & \quad \{ \text{ applying } zip \} \\
& ('a', 1) : ('b', 2) : ('c', 3) : [\,] \\
= & \quad \{ \text{ list notation } \} \\
& [('a', 1), ('b', 2), ('c', 3)]
\end{array}
$$

Note that two base cases are required in the definition of *zip*, because either of the two argument lists may be empty. As another example of recursion on multiple arguments, the library function *drop* that removes a given number of elements from the start of a list is defined as follows:

$$
\begin{array}{lcl}
drop & :: & Int \to [a] \to [a] \\
drop\ 0\ xs & = & xs \\
drop\ (n+1)\ [\,] & = & [\,] \\
drop\ (n+1)\ (\_:xs) & = & drop\ n\ xs
\end{array}
$$

Again, two base cases are required, one for removing zero elements, and one for attempting to remove one or more elements from the empty list.

6.4 | Multiple recursion

Functions can also be defined using *multiple recursion*, in which a function is applied more than once in its own definition. For example, recall the Fibonacci sequence $0, 1, 1, 2, 3, 5, 8, 13, \ldots$, in which the first two numbers are 0 and 1, and each subsequent number is given by adding the preceding two numbers in the sequence. In Haskell, a function that calculates the nth Fibonacci number for any integer $n \geq 0$ can be defined using double recursion as follows:

$$
\begin{array}{lcl}
fibonacci & :: & Int \to Int \\
fibonacci\ 0 & = & 0 \\
fibonacci\ 1 & = & 1 \\
fibonacci\ (n+2) & = & fibonacci\ n + fibonacci\ (n+1)
\end{array}
$$

As another example, in chapter 1 we showed how to implement another well-known method of sorting a list, called quicksort:

$$
\begin{array}{lcl}
qsort & :: & Ord\ a \Rightarrow [a] \to [a] \\
qsort\ [\,] & = & [\,] \\
qsort\ (x:xs) & = & qsort\ smaller \mathbin{+\!\!+} [x] \mathbin{+\!\!+} qsort\ larger
\end{array}
$$
$$
\begin{array}{l}
\textbf{where} \\
\quad smaller = [a \mid a \leftarrow xs,\, a \leq x] \\
\quad larger = [b \mid b \leftarrow xs,\, b > x]
\end{array}
$$

That is, the empty list is already sorted, and any non-empty list can be sorted by placing its head between the two lists that result from sorting those elements of its tail that are *smaller* and *larger* than the head.

6.5 | Mutual recursion

Functions can also be defined using *mutual recursion*, in which two or more functions are all defined in terms of each other. For example, consider the library functions *even* and *odd*. For efficiency, these functions are normally defined using the remainder after dividing by two. However, for non-negative integers they can also be defined using mutual recursion:

$$
\begin{array}{lll}
even & :: & Int \to Bool \\
even\ 0 & = & True \\
even\ (n+1) & = & odd\ n \\
\\
odd & :: & Int \to Bool \\
odd\ 0 & = & False \\
odd\ (n+1) & = & even\ n
\end{array}
$$

That is, zero is even but not odd, and any strictly positive integer is even if its predecessor is odd, and odd if its predecessor is even. For example:

$$
\begin{array}{ll}
& even\ 4 \\
= & \{\ applying\ even\ \} \\
& odd\ 3 \\
= & \{\ applying\ odd\ \} \\
& even\ 2 \\
= & \{\ applying\ even\ \} \\
& odd\ 1 \\
= & \{\ applying\ odd\ \} \\
& even\ 0 \\
= & \{\ applying\ even\ \} \\
& True
\end{array}
$$

Similarly, functions that select the elements from a list at all even and odd positions (counting from zero) can be defined as follows:

$$
\begin{array}{lll}
evens & :: & [\,a\,] \to [\,a\,] \\
evens\ [\,] & = & [\,] \\
evens\ (x:xs) & = & x:odds\ xs \\
\\
odds & :: & [\,a\,] \to [\,a\,] \\
odds\ [\,] & = & [\,] \\
odds\ (\_:xs) & = & evens\ xs
\end{array}
$$

For example:

$$
\begin{array}{ll}
& evens\ \texttt{"abcde"} \\
= & \{\ applying\ evens\ \} \\
& \texttt{'a'}:odds\ \texttt{"bcde"} \\
= & \{\ applying\ odds\ \} \\
& \texttt{'a'}:evens\ \texttt{"cde"} \\
= & \{\ applying\ evens\ \} \\
& \texttt{'a'}:\texttt{'c'}:odds\ \texttt{"de"} \\
= & \{\ applying\ odds\ \} \\
& \texttt{'a'}:\texttt{'c'}:evens\ \texttt{"e"} \\
= & \{\ applying\ evens\ \} \\
& \texttt{'a'}:\texttt{'c'}:\texttt{'e'}:odds\ [\,] \\
= & \{\ applying\ odds\ \} \\
& \texttt{'a'}:\texttt{'c'}:\texttt{'e'}:[\,] \\
= & \{\ string\ notation\ \} \\
& \texttt{"ace"}
\end{array}
$$

Recall that strings in Haskell are actually constructed as lists of characters. Hence, `"abcde"` is just an abbreviation for [`'a'`, `'b'`, `'c'`, `'d'`, `'e'`].

6.6 | Advice on recursion

Defining recursive functions is like riding a bicycle: it looks easy when someone else is doing it, may seem impossible when you first try to do it yourself, but becomes simple and natural with practice. In this section we offer some advice for defining functions in general, and recursive functions in particular, using a five-step process that we introduce by means of examples.

Example – *product*

As a simple first example, we show how the definition given earlier in this chapter for the library function that calculates the *product* of a list of numbers can be constructed in a stepwise manner.

Step 1: define the type

Thinking about types is very helpful when defining functions, so it is good practice to define the type of a function prior to starting to define the function itself. In this case, we begin with the type

$$product \quad :: \quad [Int] \rightarrow Int$$

that states that *product* takes a list of integers and produces a single integer. As in this example, it is often useful to begin with a simple type, which can be refined or generalised later on as appropriate.

Step 2: enumerate the cases

For most types of argument, there are a number of standard cases to consider. For lists, the standard cases are the empty list and non-empty lists, so we can write down the following skeleton definition using pattern matching:

$$product \, [\,] \qquad =$$
$$product \, (n : ns) \quad =$$

For non-negative integers, the standard cases are 0 and $n + 1$, for logical values they are *False* and *True*, and so on. As with the type, we may need to refine the cases later on, but it is useful to begin with the standard cases.

Step 3: define the simple cases

By definition, the product of zero integers is one, because one is the identity for multiplication. Hence it is straightforward to define the empty list case:

$$product \, [\,] \qquad = \quad 1$$
$$product \, (n : ns) \quad =$$

As in this example, the simple cases often become base cases.

Step 4: define the other cases

How can we calculate the product of a non-empty list of integers? For this step, it is useful to first consider the ingredients that can be used, such as the function itself (*product*), the arguments (n and ns), and library functions of relevant types ($+$, $-$, $*$, and so on.) In this case, we simply multiply the first integer and the product of the remaining list of integers:

$$\begin{aligned} product\ [\,] &= 1 \\ product\ (n:ns) &= n*product\ ns \end{aligned}$$

As in this example, the other cases often become recursive cases.

Step 5: generalise and simplify

Once a function has been defined using the above process, it often becomes clear that it can be generalised and simplified. For example, the function *product* does not depend on the precise kind of numbers to which it is applied, so its type can be generalised from integers to any numeric type:

$$product\ ::\ Num\ a \Rightarrow [a] \to a$$

In terms of simplification, we will see in chapter 7 that the pattern of recursion used in *product* is encapsulated by a library function called *foldr*, using which *product* can be redefined by a single equation:

$$product\ =\ foldr\ (*)\ 1$$

In conclusion, our final definition for *product* is as follows:

$$\begin{aligned} product\ &::\ Num\ a \Rightarrow [a] \to a \\ product\ &=\ foldr\ (*)\ 1 \end{aligned}$$

This is precisely the definition from the standard prelude in appendix A, except that for efficiency reasons the use of *foldr* is replaced by the related library function *foldl*, which is also discussed in chapter 7.

Example – *drop*

As a more substantial example, we now show how the definition given earlier for the library function *drop* that removes a given number of elements from the start of a list can be constructed using the five-step process.

Step 1: define the type

Let us begin with a type that states that *drop* takes an integer and a list of values of some type a, and produces another list of such values:

$$drop\ ::\ Int \to [a] \to [a]$$

Note that we have made four decisions in defining this type: using integers rather than a more general numeric type, for simplicity; using currying rather than taking the arguments as a pair, for flexibility (see section 3.6); supplying the integer argument before the list argument, for readability (*drop n xs* can be read as "drop n elements from xs"); and, finally, making the function polymorphic in the type of the list elements, for generality.

Step 2: enumerate the cases

As there are two standard cases for the integer argument (0 and $n + 1$) and two for the list argument ($[\,]$ and $x:xs$), writing down a skeleton definition using pattern matching requires four cases in total:

$$
\begin{array}{ll}
drop\ 0\ [\,] & = \\
drop\ 0\ (x : xs) & = \\
drop\ (n + 1)\ [\,] & = \\
drop\ (n + 1)\ (x : xs) & = \\
\end{array}
$$

Step 3: define the simple cases

By definition, removing zero elements from the start of any list gives the same list, so it is straightforward to define the first two cases:

$$
\begin{array}{lll}
drop\ 0\ [\,] & = & [\,] \\
drop\ 0\ (x : xs) & = & x : xs \\
drop\ (n + 1)\ [\,] & = & \\
drop\ (n + 1)\ (x : xs) & = & \\
\end{array}
$$

Attempting to removing one or more elements from the empty list is invalid, so the third case could be omitted, which would result in an error being produced if this situation arises. In practice, however, we choose to avoid the production of an error by returning the empty list in this case:

$$
\begin{array}{lll}
drop\ 0\ [\,] & = & [\,] \\
drop\ 0\ (x : xs) & = & x : xs \\
drop\ (n + 1)\ [\,] & = & [\,] \\
drop\ (n + 1)\ (x : xs) & = & \\
\end{array}
$$

Step 4: define the other cases

How can we remove one or more elements from a non-empty list? By simply removing one less element from the tail of the list:

$$
\begin{array}{lll}
drop\ 0\ [\,] & = & [\,] \\
drop\ 0\ (x : xs) & = & x : xs \\
drop\ (n + 1)\ [\,] & = & [\,] \\
drop\ (n + 1)\ (x : xs) & = & drop\ n\ xs \\
\end{array}
$$

Step 5: generalise and simplify

Because the function $drop$ does not depend on the precise kind of integers to which it is applied, its type can be generalised to any integral type, of which Int and $Integer$ are the standard instances:

$$
drop\ ::\ Integral\ b \Rightarrow b \to [\,a\,] \to [\,a\,]
$$

For efficiency reasons, however, this generalisation is not in fact made in the standard prelude, as noted in section 3.9. In terms of simplification, the first two equations for $drop$ can be combined into a single equation that states that removing zero elements from any list gives the same list:

$$
\begin{array}{lll}
drop\ 0\ xs & = & xs \\
drop\ (n + 1)\ [\,] & = & [\,] \\
drop\ (n + 1)\ (x : xs) & = & drop\ n\ xs \\
\end{array}
$$

Moreover, the variable x in the last equation can be replaced by the wildcard pattern _, because this variable is not used in the body of the equation:

$$
\begin{aligned}
drop\ 0\ xs &= xs \\
drop\ (n+1)\ [\,] &= [\,] \\
drop\ (n+1)\ (\_ : xs) &= drop\ n\ xs
\end{aligned}
$$

We might similarly expect n in the second equation to be replaced by $\_$, but this would make the definition invalid, because patterns of the form $n + k$ require that n is a variable. This constraint could be avoided by replacing the entire pattern $n + 1$ in the second equation by $\_$, but this would change the behaviour of the function. For example, evaluating $drop\ (-1)\ [\,]$ would then produce the empty list whereas it currently produces an error, because $\_$ can match any integer whereas $n + 1$ only matches integers ≥ 1.

In conclusion, our final definition for $drop$ is as follows, which is precisely the definition from the standard prelude in appendix A:

$$
\begin{aligned}
drop\ &:: \quad Int \to [\,a\,] \to [\,a\,] \\
drop\ 0\ xs &= xs \\
drop\ (n+1)\ [\,] &= [\,] \\
drop\ (n+1)\ (\_ : xs) &= drop\ n\ xs
\end{aligned}
$$

Example – $init$

As a final example, let us consider how the definition for library function $init$ that removes the last element from a non-empty list can be constructed.

Step 1: define the type

We begin with a type that states that $init$ takes a list of values of some type a, and produces another list of such values:

$$
init\ :: \quad [\,a\,] \to [\,a\,]
$$

Step 2: enumerate the cases

As the empty list is not a valid argument for $init$, writing down a skeleton definition using pattern matching requires just one case:

$$
init\ (x : xs) =
$$

Step 3: define the simple cases

Whereas in the previous two examples this step was straightforward, a little more thought is required for the function $init$. By definition, however, removing the last element from a list with one element gives the empty list, so we can introduce a guard to handle this simple case:

$$
\begin{aligned}
init\ (x : xs)\ &|\ null\ xs &= [\,] \\
&|\ otherwise &=
\end{aligned}
$$

Recall that the library function $null$ decides if a list is empty or not.

Step 4: define the other cases

How can we remove the last element from a list with at least two elements? By simply retaining the head and removing the last element from the tail:

$$init \ (x : xs) \ | \ null \ xs \quad = \quad []$$
$$| \ otherwise \quad = \quad x : init \ xs$$

Step 5: generalise and simplify

The type for *init* is already as general as possible, but the definition itself can now be simplified by using pattern matching rather than guards, and by using a wildcard pattern in the first equation rather than a variable:

$$init \qquad :: \quad [a] \rightarrow [a]$$
$$init \ [\_] \qquad = \quad []$$
$$init \ (x : xs) \quad = \quad x : init \ xs$$

Again, this is precisely the definition from the standard prelude.

6.7 | Chapter remarks

The recursive definitions presented in this chapter emphasise clarity, but many can be improved in terms of efficiency, using techniques from chapters 12 and 13. The five-step process for defining functions is based upon (10).

6.8 | Exercises

1. Define the exponentiation operator ↑ for non-negative integers using the same pattern of recursion as the multiplication operator ∗, and show how 2 ↑ 3 is evaluated using your definition.

2. Using the definitions given in this chapter, show how *length* [1, 2, 3], *drop* 3 [1, 2, 3, 4, 5], and *init* [1, 2, 3] are evaluated.

3. Without looking at the definitions from the standard prelude, define the following library functions using recursion.

   - Decide if all logical values in a list are *True*:

     $$and \quad :: \quad [Bool] \rightarrow Bool$$

   - Concatenate a list of lists:

     $$concat \quad :: \quad [[a]] \rightarrow [a]$$

   - Produce a list with n identical elements:

     $$replicate \quad :: \quad Int \rightarrow a \rightarrow [a]$$

   - Select the nth element of a list:

     $$(!!) \quad :: \quad [a] \rightarrow Int \rightarrow a$$

   - Decide if a value is an element of a list:

     $$elem \quad :: \quad Eq \ a \Rightarrow a \rightarrow [a] \rightarrow Bool$$

Note: most of these functions are in fact defined in the prelude using other library functions, rather than using explicit recursion.

4. Define a recursive function $merge :: Ord\ a \Rightarrow [a] \rightarrow [a] \rightarrow [a]$ that merges two sorted lists to give a single sorted list. For example:

> $merge\ [2, 5, 6]\ [1, 3, 4]$
  $[1, 2, 3, 4, 5, 6]$

Note: your definition should not use other functions on sorted lists such as *insert* or *isort*, but should be defined using explicit recursion.

5. Using *merge*, define a recursive function $msort :: Ord\ a \Rightarrow [a] \rightarrow [a]$ that implements *merge sort*, in which the empty list and singleton lists are already sorted, and any other list is sorted by merging together the two lists that result from sorting the two halves of the list separately.

Hint: first define a function $halve :: [a] \rightarrow ([a], [a])$ that splits a list into two halves whose lengths differ by at most one.

6. Using the five-step process, define the library functions that calculate the *sum* of a list of numbers, *take* a given number of elements from the start of a list, and select the *last* element of a non-empty list.

chapter 7

Higher-order functions

In this chapter we introduce higher-order functions, which allow common programming patterns to be encapsulated as functions. We start by explaining what higher-order functions are and why they are useful, then introduce a number of standard higher-order functions for processing lists, consider function composition, and conclude by developing a string transmitter.

7.1 | Basic concepts

As we have seen in previous chapters, functions with multiple arguments are usually defined in Haskell using the notion of currying. That is, the arguments are taken one at a time by exploiting the fact that functions can return functions as results. For example, the definition

$$
\begin{aligned}
&add &&::\quad Int \to Int \to Int \\
&add\ x\ y &&=\quad x + y
\end{aligned}
$$

means

$$
\begin{aligned}
&add &&::\quad Int \to (Int \to Int) \\
&add &&=\quad \lambda x \to (\lambda y \to x + y)
\end{aligned}
$$

and states that add is a function that takes an integer x and returns a function, which in turn takes another integer y and returns their sum $x + y$. In Haskell, it is also permissible to define functions that take functions as arguments. For example, a function that takes a function and a value, and returns the result of applying the function twice to the value, can be defined as follows:

$$
\begin{aligned}
&twice &&::\quad (a \to a) \to a \to a \\
&twice\ f\ x &&=\quad f\ (f\ x)
\end{aligned}
$$

For example:

> $twice\ (*2)\ 3$
12

> *twice reverse* $[1, 2, 3]$
$[1, 2, 3]$

Moreover, because *twice* is a curried function, it can be partially applied with just one argument to build other useful functions. For example, a function that quadruples a number is given by *twice* (∗2), and the fact that reversing a (finite) list twice has no effect is captured by the equation *twice reverse = id*, where *id* is the identity function defined by $id \; x = x$.

Formally speaking, a function that takes a function as an argument or returns a function as a result is called *higher-order*. In practice, however, because the term curried already exists for returning functions as results, the term higher-order is often just used for taking functions as arguments. It is this latter interpretation that is the subject of this chapter.

Using higher-order functions considerably increases the power of Haskell, by allowing common programming patterns to be encapsulated as functions within the language itself. More generally, higher-order functions can be used to define "domain-specific" languages within Haskell. For example, in this chapter we present a simple language for processing lists, and in chapters 8 and 9 we do the same for building parsers and interactive programs.

7.2 | Processing lists

The standard prelude defines a number of useful higher-order functions for processing lists. For example, the function *map* applies a function to all elements of a list, and can be defined using a list comprehension as follows:

$$
\begin{aligned}
map & \quad :: \quad (a \to b) \to [a] \to [b] \\
map \; f \; xs & \quad = \quad [f \; x \mid x \leftarrow xs]
\end{aligned}
$$

That is, *map f xs* returns the list of all values $f \; x$ such that x is an element of the list *xs*. For example, we have:

> *map* (+1) $[1, 3, 5, 7]$
$[2, 4, 6, 8]$

> *map isDigit* $['a', '1', 'b', '2']$
$[\mathit{False}, \mathit{True}, \mathit{False}, \mathit{True}]$

> *map reverse* ["abc", "def", "ghi"]
["cba", "fed", "ihg"]

There are three further points to note about *map*. First of all, it is a polymorphic function that can be applied to lists of any type, as are most higher-order functions on lists. Secondly, it can be applied to itself to process nested lists. For example, the function *map* (*map* (+1)) increments each number in a list of lists of numbers, as shown in the following calculation:

$$
\begin{aligned}
& map \; (map \; (+1)) \; [[1, 2, 3], [4, 5]] \\
= & \quad \{ \text{ applying the outer } map \} \\
& [map \; (+1) \; [1, 2, 3], \; map \; (+1) \; [4, 5]]
\end{aligned}
$$

$$= \quad \{ \text{applying } map \}$$
$$[[2, 3, 4], [5, 6]]$$

And, finally, the function map can also be defined using recursion:

$$map \ f \ [\,] \qquad = \quad [\,]$$
$$map \ f \ (x : xs) \quad = \quad f \ x : map \ f \ xs$$

That is, applying a function to all elements of the empty list gives the empty list, while for a non-empty list the function is simply applied to the head of the list, and we then proceed to apply the function to all elements of the tail. The original definition for map using a list comprehension is simpler, but the recursive definition is preferable for reasoning purposes (see chapter 13.)

Another useful library function is *filter*, which selects all elements of a list that satisfy a predicate, where a *predicate* (or property) is a function that returns a logical value. As with map, the function *filter* also has a simple definition using a list comprehension:

$$filter \qquad :: \quad (a \rightarrow Bool) \rightarrow [a] \rightarrow [a]$$
$$filter \ p \ xs \quad = \quad [x \mid x \leftarrow xs, p \ x]$$

That is, $filter \ p \ xs$ returns the list of all values x such that x is an element of the list xs and the value of $p \ x$ is *True*. For example:

$$> \ filter \ even \ [1 .. 10]$$
$$[2, 4, 6, 8, 10]$$

$$> \ filter \ (>5) \ [1 .. 10]$$
$$[6, 7, 8, 9, 10]$$

$$> \ filter \ (\neq ' \ ') \ \texttt{"abc def ghi"}$$
$$\texttt{"abcdefghi"}$$

As with map, the function *filter* can be applied to lists of any type, and can be defined using recursion for the purposes of reasoning:

$$filter \ p \ [\,] \qquad\qquad = \quad [\,]$$
$$filter \ p \ (x : xs) \mid p \ x \quad = \quad x : filter \ p \ xs$$
$$\qquad\qquad \mid otherwise \quad = \quad filter \ p \ xs$$

That is, selecting all elements that satisfy a predicate from the empty list gives the empty list, while for a non-empty list the result depends upon whether the head satisfies the predicate. If it does then the head is retained and we then proceed to filter elements from the tail of the list, otherwise the head is discarded and we simply filter elements from the tail.

The functions map and *filter* are often used together in programs, with *filter* being used to select certain elements from a list, each of which is then transformed using map. For example, a function that returns the sum of the squares of the even integers from a list could be defined as follows:

$$sumsqreven \qquad :: \quad [Int] \rightarrow Int$$
$$sumsqreven \ ns \quad = \quad sum \ (map \ (\uparrow 2) \ (filter \ even \ ns))$$

We conclude this section by illustrating a number of other higher-order functions for processing lists that are defined in the standard prelude.

- Decide if all elements of a list satisfy a predicate:

  > *all even* [2, 4, 6, 8]
  True

- Decide if any element of a list satisfies a predicate:

  > *any odd* [2, 4, 6, 8]
  False

- Select elements from a list while they satisfy a predicate:

  > *takeWhile isLower* "abc def"
  "abc"

- Remove elements from a list while they satisfy a predicate:

  > *dropWhile isLower* "abc def"
  " def"

7.3 | The *foldr* function

Many functions that take a list as their argument can be defined using the following simple pattern of recursion on lists:

$$
\begin{aligned}
f\,[\,] \quad &= \quad v \\
f\,(x : xs) \quad &= \quad x \oplus f\,xs
\end{aligned}
$$

That is, the function maps the empty list to a value v, and any non-empty list to an operator $\oplus$ applied to the head of the list and the result of recursively processing the tail. For example, a number of familiar library functions on lists can be defined using this pattern:

$$
\begin{aligned}
sum\,[\,] \quad &= \quad 0 \\
sum\,(x : xs) \quad &= \quad x + sum\,xs \\
product\,[\,] \quad &= \quad 1 \\
product\,(x : xs) \quad &= \quad x * product\,xs \\
or\,[\,] \quad &= \quad False \\
or\,(x : xs) \quad &= \quad x \vee or\,xs \\
and\,[\,] \quad &= \quad True \\
and\,(x : xs) \quad &= \quad x \wedge and\,xs
\end{aligned}
$$

The higher-order library function *foldr* (abbreviating "fold right") encapsulates this pattern of recursion for defining functions on lists, with the operator $\oplus$ and the value v as arguments. For example, using *foldr* the four definitions above can be rewritten more compactly as follows:

$$sum \quad = \quad foldr \ (+) \ 0$$
$$product \ = \quad foldr \ (*) \ 1$$
$$or \quad = \quad foldr \ (\lor) \ False$$
$$and \quad = \quad foldr \ (\land) \ True$$

(Recall that operators must be parenthesised when used as arguments.) These new definitions could also include explicit list arguments, as in $sum \ xs = foldr \ (+) \ 0 \ xs$, but we prefer the above definitions in which these arguments are made implicit using partial application because they are simpler.

The *foldr* function itself is defined using recursion:

$$foldr \qquad\qquad :: \quad (a \to b \to b) \to b \to [a] \to b$$
$$foldr \ f \ v \ [] \qquad = \quad v$$
$$foldr \ f \ v \ (x : xs) \ = \quad f \ x \ (foldr \ f \ v \ xs)$$

That is, the function *foldr f v* maps the empty list to the value v, and any non-empty list to the function f applied to the head of the list and the recursively processed tail. In practice, however, it is best to think of the behaviour of *foldr f v* in a non-recursive manner, as simply replacing each cons operator in a list by the function f, and the empty list at the end by the value v. For example, applying the function *foldr* $(+)$ 0 to the list

$$1 : (2 : (3 : []))$$

gives the result

$$1 + (2 + (3 + 0))$$

in which : and [] have been replaced by + and 0, respectively. Hence, the definition $sum = foldr \ (+) \ 0$ states that summing a list of numbers amounts to replacing each cons by addition and the empty list by zero.

Even though *foldr* encapsulates a simple pattern of recursion, it can be used to define many more functions than might first be expected. First of all, recall the following definition for the library function *length*:

$$length \qquad\qquad :: \quad [a] \to Int$$
$$length \ [] \qquad = \quad 0$$
$$length \ (\_ : xs) \ = \quad 1 + length \ xs$$

For example, applying *length* to the list

$$1 : (2 : (3 : []))$$

gives the result

$$1 + (1 + (1 + 0))$$

That is, calculating the length of a list amounts to replacing each cons by the function that adds one to its second argument, and the empty list by zero. Hence, the definition for *length* can be rewritten using *foldr*:

$$length \quad = \quad foldr \ (\lambda\_ \ n \to 1 + n) \ 0$$

Now let us consider the library function that reverses a list, which can be defined using explicit recursion as follows:

$$reverse \quad :: \quad [a] \to [a]$$
$$reverse\ [\,] \quad = \quad [\,]$$
$$reverse\ (x:xs) \quad = \quad reverse\ xs \mathbin{+\!\!+} [x]$$

For example, applying *reverse* to the list

$$1:(2:(3:[\,]))$$

gives the result

$$(([\,] \mathbin{+\!\!+} [3]) \mathbin{+\!\!+} [2]) \mathbin{+\!\!+} [1]$$

It is perhaps not immediately clear from the definition, or the example, how *reverse* can be defined using *foldr*. However, if we define a function $snoc\ x\ xs = xs \mathbin{+\!\!+} [x]$ that adds a new element at the end of a list rather than at the start ("snoc" is cons backwards), then *reverse* can be redefined as

$$reverse\ [\,] \quad = \quad [\,]$$
$$reverse\ (x:xs) \quad = \quad snoc\ x\ (reverse\ xs)$$

from which a definition using *foldr* is then immediate:

$$reverse \quad = \quad foldr\ snoc\ [\,]$$

That is, reversing a list amounts to replacing each cons by *snoc* and the empty list by itself. The append operator $\mathbin{+\!\!+}$ used in the definition of *snoc* can itself be defined in a particularly compact manner using *foldr*:

$$(\mathbin{+\!\!+}\ ys) \quad = \quad foldr\ (:)\ ys$$

That is, appending *ys* to the end of a list amounts to replacing each cons in the list by itself, and the empty list at the end by *ys*.

We conclude this section by noting that the name fold *right* reflects the use of an operator that is assumed to associate to the right. For example, evaluating $foldr\ (+)\ 0\ [1, 2, 3]$ gives the result $1 + (2 + (3 + 0))$, in which the bracketing specifies that addition here is assumed to associate to the right. More generally, the behaviour of *foldr* can be summarised as follows:

$$foldr\ (\oplus)\ v\ [x_0, x_1, \cdots, x_n] \quad = \quad x_0 \oplus (x_1 \oplus (\cdots (x_n \oplus v) \cdots))$$

7.4 | The *foldl* function

It is also possible to define recursive functions on lists using an operator that is assumed to associate to the left. For example, the function *sum* can be redefined in this manner by using an auxiliary function *sum'* that takes an extra argument *v* that is used to accumulate the final result:

$$sum \quad = \quad sum'\ 0$$
$$\textbf{where}$$
$$sum'\ v\ [\,] = v$$
$$sum'\ v\ (x:xs) = sum'\ (v + x)\ xs$$

For example:

$$sum\ [1, 2, 3]$$

$$
\begin{aligned}
&= \quad \{ \text{applying } sum \} \\
&sum'\ 0\ [1, 2, 3] \\
&= \quad \{ \text{applying } sum' \} \\
&sum'\ (0 + 1)\ [2, 3] \\
&= \quad \{ \text{applying } sum' \} \\
&sum'\ ((0 + 1) + 2)\ [3] \\
&= \quad \{ \text{applying } sum' \} \\
&sum'\ (((0 + 1) + 2) + 3)\ [\,] \\
&= \quad \{ \text{applying } sum' \} \\
&((0 + 1) + 2) + 3 \\
&= \quad \{ \text{applying } + \} \\
&6
\end{aligned}
$$

The bracketing in this calculation specifies that addition is now assumed to associate to the left. In practice, however, the order of association does not affect the value of the result in this case, because addition is *associative*. That is, $x + (y + z) = (x + y) + z$ for any numbers x, y, and z.

Generalising from the *sum* example, many functions on lists can be defined using the following simple pattern of recursion:

$$
\begin{aligned}
f\ v\ [\,] &= v \\
f\ v\ (x : xs) &= f\ (v \oplus x)\ xs
\end{aligned}
$$

That is, the function maps the empty list to the *accumulator* value v, and any non-empty list to the result of recursively processing the tail using a new accumulator value obtained by applying an operator $\oplus$ to the current value and the head of the list. The higher-order library function *foldl* (abbreviating "fold left") encapsulates this pattern of recursion, with the operator $\oplus$ and the accumulator v as arguments. For example, using *foldl* the above definition for *sum* can be rewritten more compactly as follows:

$$
sum \quad = \quad foldl\ (+)\ 0
$$

Similarly, we have:

$$
\begin{aligned}
product &= \quad foldl\ (*)\ 1 \\
or &= \quad foldl\ (\vee)\ False \\
and &= \quad foldl\ (\wedge)\ True
\end{aligned}
$$

The other *foldr* examples from the previous section can also be redefined using *foldl*, by supplying the appropriate operators:

$$
\begin{aligned}
length &= \quad foldl\ (\lambda n\ \_ \to n + 1)\ 0 \\
reverse &= \quad foldl\ (\lambda xs\ x \to x : xs)\ [\,] \\
(xs{+}{+}) &= \quad foldl\ (\lambda ys\ y \to ys {+}{+} [y])\ xs
\end{aligned}
$$

For example, with these new definitions:

$$
\begin{aligned}
length\ [1, 2, 3] &= \quad ((0 + 1) + 1) + 1 \\
reverse\ [1, 2, 3] &= \quad 3 : (2 : (1 : [\,])) \\
[1, 2, 3] {+}{+} [4, 5] &= \quad ([1, 2, 3] {+}{+} [4]) {+}{+} [5]
\end{aligned}
$$

When a function can be defined using both *foldr* and *foldl*, as in the above examples, the choice of which definition is preferable is usually made on grounds of efficiency and requires careful consideration of the evaluation mechanism underlying Haskell, which is discussed in chapter 12.

The *foldl* function itself is defined using recursion:

$$
\begin{aligned}
foldl & \quad :: \quad (a \to b \to a) \to a \to [b] \to a \\
foldl\ f\ v\ [\,] & \quad = \quad v \\
foldl\ f\ v\ (x:xs) & \quad = \quad foldl\ f\ (f\ v\ x)\ xs
\end{aligned}
$$

In practice, however, as with *foldr* it is best to think of the behaviour of *foldl* in a non-recursive manner, in terms of an operator $\oplus$ that is assumed to associate to the left, as summarised by the following equation:

$$
foldl\ (\oplus)\ v\ [x_0, x_1, \cdots, x_n] \quad = \quad (\cdots ((v \oplus x_0) \oplus x_1) \cdots) \oplus x_n
$$

7.5 | The composition operator

The higher-order library operator $\circ$ returns the *composition* of two functions as a single function, and can be defined as follows:

$$
\begin{aligned}
(\circ) & \quad :: \quad (b \to c) \to (a \to b) \to (a \to c) \\
f \circ g & \quad = \quad \lambda x \to f\ (g\ x)
\end{aligned}
$$

That is, $f \circ g$ (read as "f composed with g") is the function that takes an argument x, applies the function g to this argument, and applies the function f to the result. This operator could also be defined by $(f \circ g)\ x = f\ (g\ x)$. However, we prefer the above definition in which the x argument is shunted to the body of the definition using a lambda expression, because it makes explicit the idea that composition returns a function as its result.

Composition can be used to simplify nested function applications, by reducing parentheses and avoiding the need to explicitly refer to the initial argument. For example, using composition the definitions

$$
\begin{aligned}
odd\ n & \quad = \quad \neg\ (even\ n) \\
twice\ f\ x & \quad = \quad f\ (f\ x) \\
sumsqreven\ ns & \quad = \quad sum\ (map\ (\uparrow 2)\ (filter\ even\ ns))
\end{aligned}
$$

can be rewritten more simply:

$$
\begin{aligned}
odd & \quad = \quad \neg \circ even \\
twice\ f & \quad = \quad f \circ f \\
sumsqreven & \quad = \quad sum \circ map\ (\uparrow 2) \circ filter\ even
\end{aligned}
$$

The last definition exploits the fact that composition is associative. That is, $f \circ (g \circ h) = (f \circ g) \circ h$ for any functions f, g, and h of the appropriate types. Hence, in a composition of three of more functions, as in *sumsqreven*, there is no need to include parentheses to indicate the order of association, because associativity ensures that this does not affect the result.

Composition also has an identity, given by the *identity function*:

$$id \quad :: \quad a \to a$$
$$id \quad = \quad \lambda x \to x$$

That is, id is the function that simply returns its argument unchanged, and has the property that $id \circ f = f$ and $f \circ id = f$ for any function f. The identity function is often useful when reasoning about programs, and also provides a suitable starting point for a sequence of compositions. For example, the composition of a list of functions can be defined as follows:

$$compose \quad :: \quad [a \to a] \to (a \to a)$$
$$compose \quad = \quad foldr \, (\circ) \, id$$

7.6 | String transmitter

We conclude this chapter with an extended example. Consider the problem of simulating the transmission of a string using zeros and ones. More precisely, we seek to define a function that converts a string into a list of zeros and ones, together with a function that performs the opposite conversion.

Binary numbers

As a consequence of having ten fingers, people normally find it most convenient to use numbers written in base-ten or *decimal* notation. A decimal number is sequence of digits in the range zero to nine, in which the rightmost digit has a weight of one, and successive digits as we move to the left in the number increase in weight by a factor of ten. For example, the decimal number 2345 can be understood in these terms as follows:

$$2345 \quad = \quad (1000 * 2) + (100 * 3) + (10 * 4) + (1 * 5)$$

That is, 2345 represents the sum of the products of the weights 1000,100,10,1 with the digits 2,3,4,5, which evaluates to the integer 2345.

In contrast, computers normally find it more convenient to use numbers written in the more primitive base-two or *binary* notation. A binary number is a sequence of zeros and ones, called binary digits or *bits*, in which successive bits as we move to the left increase in weight by a factor of two. For example, the binary number 1101 can be understood as follows:

$$1101 \quad = \quad (8 * 1) + (4 * 1) + (2 * 0) + (1 * 1)$$

That is, 1101 represents the sum of the products of the weights 8,4,2,1 with the bits 1,1,0,1, which evaluates to the integer 13.

To simplify the definition of certain functions, we assume for the remainder of this example that binary numbers are written in *reverse* order to normal. For example, 1101 would now be written as 1011, with successive bits as we move to the right increasing in weight by a factor of two:

$$1011 \quad = \quad (1 * 1) + (2 * 0) + (4 * 1) + (8 * 1)$$

Base conversion

To make the types of the functions that we define more meaningful, we declare a type for bits as a synonym for the type of integers:

$$\textbf{type } Bit \quad = \quad Int$$

A binary number, represented as a list of bits, can be converted into an integer by simply evaluating the required weighted sum:

$$
\begin{aligned}
bin2int \quad &:: \quad [\,Bit\,] \rightarrow Int \\
bin2int \ bits \quad &= \quad sum\,[\,w * b \mid (w,\,b) \leftarrow zip\ weights\ bits\,] \\
&\qquad \textbf{where}\ weights = iterate\ (*2)\ 1
\end{aligned}
$$

The higher-order library function *iterate* produces a list by applying a function an increasing number of times to a value:

$$iterate\ f\ x \quad = \quad [\,x, f\ x, f\ (f\ x), f\ (f\ (f\ x)), \cdots]$$

Hence the expression *iterate* $(*2)$ 1 used within the definition of *bin2int* produces the list of weights $[1, 2, 4, 8, \cdots]$. This list is notionally infinite, but under lazy evaluation as discussed in chapter 12, only as many elements as required by the context in which it is used — in this case zipping with the list of bits — will actually be produced. For example:

```
>  bin2int [1, 0, 1, 1]
13
```

There is, however, a simpler way to define *bin2int*, which can be revealed with the aid of a little algebra. Consider an arbitrary four-bit binary number $[\,a, b, c, d\,]$. Applying *bin2int* to this list will produce the weighted sum

$$(1 * a) + (2 * b) + (4 * c) + (8 * d)$$

which can be restructured as follows:

$$
\begin{aligned}
&(1 * a) + (2 * b) + (4 * c) + (8 * d) \\
= \quad &\{\ \text{simplifying } 1 * a\ \} \\
&a + (2 * b) + (4 * c) + (8 * d) \\
= \quad &\{\ \text{factoring out } 2 *\ \} \\
&a + 2 * (b + (2 * c) + (4 * d)) \\
= \quad &\{\ \text{factoring out } 2 *\ \} \\
&a + 2 * (b + 2 * (c + (2 * d))) \\
= \quad &\{\ \text{complicating } d\ \} \\
&a + 2 * (b + 2 * (c + 2 * (d + (2 * 0))))
\end{aligned}
$$

The final result shows that converting a list of bits $[\,a, b, c, d\,]$ into an integer amounts to replacing each cons by the function that adds its first argument to twice its second argument, and replacing the empty list by zero. More generally, we conclude that *bin2int* can be rewritten using *foldr*:

$$bin2int \quad = \quad foldr\ (\lambda x\ y \rightarrow x + 2 * y)\ 0$$

Now let us consider the opposite conversion, from a non-negative integer into a binary number. This can be achieved by repeatedly dividing the integer by two and taking the remainder, until the integer becomes zero. For example, starting with the integer 13 we proceed as follows:

$$
\begin{array}{llllll}
13 & \text{divided by} & 2 & = & 6 & \text{remainder} & 1 \\
6 & \text{divided by} & 2 & = & 3 & \text{remainder} & 0 \\
3 & \text{divided by} & 2 & = & 1 & \text{remainder} & 1 \\
1 & \text{divided by} & 2 & = & 0 & \text{remainder} & 1
\end{array}
$$

The sequence of remainders, 1011, provides the binary representation of the integer 13. It is easy to implement this procedure using recursion:

$$
\begin{aligned}
int2bin & \quad :: \quad Int \rightarrow [Bit] \\
int2bin\ 0 & \quad = \quad [\,] \\
int2bin\ n & \quad = \quad n\ `mod`\ 2 : int2bin\ (n\ `div`\ 2)
\end{aligned}
$$

For example:

```
> int2bin 13
[1, 0, 1, 1]
```

We will ensure that all our binary numbers have the same length, eight bits, by using a function *make8* that truncates or extends a binary number as appropriate to make it precisely eight bits:

$$
\begin{aligned}
make8 & \quad :: \quad [Bit] \rightarrow [Bit] \\
make8\ bits & \quad = \quad take\ 8\ (bits \mathbin{+\!\!+} repeat\ 0)
\end{aligned}
$$

The library function *repeat* produces an infinite list of copies of a value, but once again lazy evaluation ensures that only as many elements as required by the context will actually be produced. For example:

```
> make8 [1, 0, 1, 1]
[1, 0, 1, 1, 0, 0, 0, 0]
```

Transmission

We can now define a function that encodes a string of characters as a list of bits by converting each character into a Unicode number, converting each such number into an eight-bit binary number, and concatenating each of these numbers together to produce a list of bits. Using the higher-order functions *map* and composition, this conversion can be implemented as follows:

$$
\begin{aligned}
encode & \quad :: \quad String \rightarrow [Bit] \\
encode & \quad = \quad concat \circ map\ (make8 \circ int2bin \circ ord)
\end{aligned}
$$

For example:

```
> encode "abc"
[1, 0, 0, 0, 0, 1, 1, 0, 0, 1, 0, 0, 0, 1, 1, 0, 1, 1, 0, 0, 0, 1, 1, 0]
```

To decode a list of bits produced using *encode*, we first define a function *chop8* that chops such a list up into eight-bit binary numbers:

$$
\begin{aligned}
chop8 & \quad :: \quad [Bit] \rightarrow [[Bit]] \\
chop8\ [\,] & \quad = \quad [\,] \\
chop8\ bits & \quad = \quad take\ 8\ bits : chop8\ (drop\ 8\ bits)
\end{aligned}
$$

It is now easy to define a function that decodes a list of bits as a string of characters by chopping the list up, and converting each resulting binary number into a Unicode number and then a character:

$$
\begin{aligned}
decode &:: [Bit] \to String \\
decode &= map\,(chr \circ bin2int) \circ chop8
\end{aligned}
$$

For example:

```
> decode [1, 0, 0, 0, 0, 1, 1, 0, 0, 1, 0, 0, 0, 1, 1, 0, 1, 1, 0, 0, 0, 1, 1, 0]
"abc"
```

Finally, we define a function *transmit* that simulates the transmission of a string of characters as a list of bits, using a perfect communication channel that we model using the identity function:

$$
\begin{aligned}
transmit &:: String \to String \\
transmit &= decode \circ channel \circ encode \\
channel &:: [Bit] \to [Bit] \\
channel &= id
\end{aligned}
$$

For example:

```
> transmit "higher-order functions are easy"
"higher-order functions are easy"
```

7.7 | Chapter remarks

Further applications of higher-order functions, including the production of computer music, financial contracts, graphical images, hardware descriptions, logic programs, and pretty printers can be found in *The Fun of Programming* (7). A more in-depth tutorial on *foldr* is given in (14).

7.8 | Exercises

1. Show how the list comprehension $[f\ x \mid x \leftarrow xs, p\ x]$ can be re-expressed using the higher-order functions *map* and *filter*.

2. Without looking at the definitions from the standard prelude, define the higher-order functions *all*, *any*, *takeWhile*, and *dropWhile*.

3. Redefine the functions *map f* and *filter p* using *foldr*.

4. Using *foldl*, define a function $dec2int :: [Int] \to Int$ that converts a decimal number into an integer. For example:

```
> dec2int [2, 3, 4, 5]
2345
```

5. Explain why the following definition is invalid:

$$
sumsqreven = compose\,[sum, map\,(\uparrow 2), filter\ even]
$$

6. Without looking at the standard prelude, define the higher-order library function *curry* that converts a function on pairs into a curried function, and, conversely, the function *uncurry* that converts a curried function with two arguments into a function on pairs.

Hint: first write down the types of the two functions.

7. A higher-order function *unfold* that encapsulates a simple pattern of recursion for producing a list can be defined as follows:

$$
\begin{aligned}
\textit{unfold } p \; h \; t \; x \mid p \; x \quad &= \quad [\,] \\
\mid \textit{otherwise} \quad &= \quad h \; x : \textit{unfold } p \; h \; t \; (t \; x)
\end{aligned}
$$

That is, the function *unfold p h t* produces the empty list if the predicate p is true of the argument, and otherwise produces a non-empty list by applying the function h to give the head, and the function t to generate another argument that is recursively processed in the same way to produce the tail of the list. For example, the function *int2bin* can be rewritten more compactly using *unfold* as follows:

$$
\textit{int2bin} \quad = \quad \textit{unfold } (== 0) \; (`mod`2) \; (`div`2)
$$

Redefine the functions *chop8*, *map f* and *iterate f* using *unfold*.

8. Modify the string transmitter program to detect simple transmission errors using parity bits. That is, each eight-bit binary number produced during encoding is extended with a parity bit, set to one if the number contains an odd number of ones, and to zero otherwise. In turn, each resulting nine-bit binary number consumed during decoding is checked to ensure that its parity bit is correct, with the parity bit being discarded if this is the case, and a parity error reported otherwise.

Hint: the library function *error* :: *String* $\rightarrow$ *a* terminates evaluation and displays the given string as an error message.

9. Test your new string transmitter program from the previous exercise using a faulty communication channel that forgets the first bit, which can be modelled using the *tail* function on lists of bits.

chapter 8

Functional parsers

In this chapter we show how Haskell can be used to program simple parsers. We start by explaining what parsers are and why they are useful, show how parsers can naturally be viewed as functions, define a number of basic parsers and higher-order functions for combining parsers in various ways, and conclude by developing a parser for arithmetic expressions.

8.1 | Parsers

A *parser* is a program that takes a string of characters, and produces some form of tree that makes the syntactic structure of the string explicit. For example, given the string $2 * 3 + 4$, a parser for arithmetic expressions might produce a tree of the following form, in which the numbers appear at the leaves of the tree, and the operators appear at the branches:

The structure of this tree makes explicit that $+$ and $*$ are operators with two arguments, and that $*$ has higher priority than $+$.

Parsers are an important topic in computing, because most real-life programs use a parser to pre-process their input. For example, a calculator program parses numeric expressions prior to evaluating them, the Hugs system parses Haskell programs prior to executing them, and a web browser parses hypertext documents prior to displaying them. In each case, making the structure of the input explicit considerably simplifies its further processing. For example, once a numeric expression has been parsed into a tree structure such as in the example above, evaluating the expression is straightforward.

8.2 | The parser type

In Haskell, a parser can naturally be viewed directly as a function that takes a string and produces a tree. Hence, given a suitable type *Tree* of trees, the notion of a parser can be represented as a function of type *String* → *Tree*, which we abbreviate as *Parser* using the following declaration:

$$\textbf{type } Parser \quad = \quad String \rightarrow Tree$$

In general, however, a parser might not always consume its entire argument string. For example, a parser for numbers might be applied to a string comprising a number followed by a word. For this reason, we generalise our type for parsers to also return any unconsumed part of the argument string:

$$\textbf{type } Parser \quad = \quad String \rightarrow (Tree, String)$$

Similarly, a parser might not always succeed. For example, a parser for numbers might be applied to a string comprising a word. To handle this, we further generalise our type for parsers to return a list of results, with the convention that the empty list denotes failure, and a singleton list denotes success:

$$\textbf{type } Parser \quad = \quad String \rightarrow [(Tree, String)]$$

Returning a list also opens up the possibility of returning more than one result if the argument string can be parsed in more than one way. For simplicity, however, we only consider parsers that return at most one result.

Finally, different parsers will likely return different kinds of trees, or more generally, any kind of value. For example, a parser for numbers might return an integer value. Hence, it is useful to abstract from the specific type *Tree* of result values, and make this into a parameter of the *Parser* type:

$$\textbf{type } Parser \; a \quad = \quad String \rightarrow [(a, String)]$$

In summary, this declaration states that a parser of type *a* is a function that takes an input string and produces a list of results, each of which is a pair comprising a result value of type *a* and an output string. Alternatively, the parser type can also be read as a rhyme in the style of Dr Seuss!

> *A parser for things*
> *Is a function from strings*
> *To lists of pairs*
> *Of things and strings*

8.3 | Basic parsers

We now define three basic parsers that will be used as the building blocks for all other parsers. First of all, the parser *return v* always succeeds with the result value *v*, without consuming any of the input string:

$$
\begin{aligned}
return \quad &:: \quad a \rightarrow Parser \; a \\
return \; v \quad &= \quad \lambda inp \rightarrow [(v, inp)]
\end{aligned}
$$

This function could equally well be defined by $return\ v\ inp = [(v, inp)]$. However, we prefer the above definition in which the second argument inp is shunted to the body of the definition using a lambda expression, because it makes explicit that $return$ is a function that takes a single argument and returns a parser, as expressed by the type $a \rightarrow Parser\ a$.

Whereas $return\ v$ always succeeds, the dual parser $failure$ always fails, regardless of the contents of the input string:

$$
\begin{array}{lll}
failure & :: & Parser\ a \\
failure & = & \lambda inp \rightarrow [\,] \\
\end{array}
$$

Our final basic parser is $item$, which fails if the input string is empty, and succeeds with the first character as the result value otherwise:

$$
\begin{array}{lll}
item & :: & Parser\ Char \\
item & = & \lambda inp \rightarrow \textbf{case}\ inp\ \textbf{of} \\
& & \qquad [\,] \rightarrow [\,] \\
& & \qquad (x : xs) \rightarrow [(x, xs)] \\
\end{array}
$$

The **case** mechanism of Haskell used in this definition allows pattern matching to be used in the body of a definition, in this example by matching the string inp against two patterns to choose between two possible results. The **case** mechanism is not used much in this book, but can sometimes be useful.

Because parsers are functions, they could be applied to a string using normal function application, but we prefer to abstract from the representation of parsers by defining our own application function:

$$
\begin{array}{lll}
parse & :: & Parser\ a \rightarrow String \rightarrow [(a, String)] \\
parse\ p\ inp & = & p\ inp \\
\end{array}
$$

Using $parse$, we conclude this section with some examples that illustrate the behaviour of the three basic parsers defined above:

```
> parse (return 1) "abc"
[(1, "abc")]


> parse failure "abc"
[]


> parse item ""
[]


> parse item "abc"
[('a', "bc")]
```

8.4 | Sequencing

Perhaps the simplest way of combining two parsers is to apply one after the other in sequence, with the output string returned by the first parser becoming the input string to the second. But how should the result values from the two parsers be handled? One approach would be to combine the two values as a pair, using a sequencing operator for parsers with the following type:

$$Parser\ a \rightarrow Parser\ b \rightarrow Parser\ (a, b)$$

In practice, however, it turns out to be more convenient to combine the sequencing of parsers with the processing of their result values, by means of a sequencing operator $\ggg$ (read as "then") defined as follows:

$$
\begin{aligned}
(\ggg) \quad &:: \quad Parser\ a \rightarrow (a \rightarrow Parser\ b) \rightarrow Parser\ b \\
p \ggg f \quad &= \quad \lambda inp \rightarrow \textbf{case}\ parse\ p\ inp\ \textbf{of} \\
&\qquad\qquad\qquad [\,] \rightarrow [\,] \\
&\qquad\qquad\qquad [(v,\ out)] \rightarrow parse\ (f\ v)\ out
\end{aligned}
$$

That is, the parser $p \ggg f$ fails if the application of the parser p to the input string fails, and otherwise applies the function f to the result value to give a second parser, which is then applied to the output string to give the final result. In this manner, the result value produced by the first parser is made directly available for processing by the second.

A typical parser built using $\ggg$ has the following structure:

$$
\begin{aligned}
&p1 \ggg \lambda v1 \rightarrow \\
&p2 \ggg \lambda v2 \rightarrow \\
&\quad\vdots \\
&pn \ggg \lambda vn \rightarrow \\
&return\ (f\ v1\ v2 \ldots vn)
\end{aligned}
$$

That is, apply the parser $p1$ and call its result value $v1$; then apply the parser $p2$ and call its result value $v2$; ... ; then apply the parser pn and call its result value vn; and, finally, combine all the results into a single value by applying the function f. Haskell provides a special syntax for such parsers, allowing them to be expressed in the following, more appealing, form:

$$
\begin{aligned}
&\textbf{do}\ v1 \leftarrow p1 \\
&\quad\ v2 \leftarrow p2 \\
&\quad\ \vdots \\
&\quad\ vn \leftarrow pn \\
&\quad\ return\ (f\ v1\ v2 \ldots vn)
\end{aligned}
$$

As with list comprehensions, the expressions $vi \leftarrow pi$ are called *generators*. If the result value produced by a generator $vi \leftarrow pi$ is not required, the generator can be abbreviated simply by pi. Note also that the layout rule applies to the **do** notation for sequencing parsers, in the sense that each parser in the sequence must begin in precisely the same column.

For example, a parser that consumes three characters, discards the second, and returns the first and third as a pair can now be defined as follows:

$$
\begin{aligned}
&p \quad :: \quad Parser\ (Char,\ Char) \\
&p \quad = \quad \textbf{do}\ x \leftarrow item \\
&\qquad\qquad\ item \\
&\qquad\qquad\ y \leftarrow item \\
&\qquad\qquad\ return\ (x,\ y)
\end{aligned}
$$

Note that p only succeeds if every parser in its defining sequence succeeds, which requires at least three characters in the input string:

```
> parse p "abcdef"
[(('a','c'),"def")]
```

```
> parse p "ab"
[]
```

8.5 | Choice

Another natural way of combining two parsers is to apply the first parser to the input string, and if this fails to apply the second instead. Such a choice operator +++ (read as "or else") can be defined as follows:

$$
\begin{array}{lll}
(+\!+\!+) & :: & Parser\ a \rightarrow Parser\ a \rightarrow Parser\ a \\
p +\!+\!+ q & = & \lambda inp \rightarrow \textbf{case } parse\ p\ inp\ \textbf{of} \\
& & \qquad\qquad [\,] \rightarrow parse\ q\ inp \\
& & \qquad\qquad [(v, out)] \rightarrow [(v, out)]
\end{array}
$$

For example:

```
> parse (item +++ return 'd') "abc"
[('a',"bc")]
```

```
> parse (failure +++ return 'd') "abc"
[('d',"abc")]
```

```
> parse (failure +++ failure) "abc"
[]
```

8.6 | Derived primitives

Using the three basic parsers together with sequencing and choice, we can now define a number of other useful parsing primitives. First of all, we define a parser $sat\ p$ for single characters that satisfy the predicate p:

$$
\begin{array}{lll}
sat & :: & (Char \rightarrow Bool) \rightarrow Parser\ Char \\
sat\ p & = & \textbf{do } x \leftarrow item \\
& & \qquad \textbf{if } p\ x\ \textbf{then } return\ x\ \textbf{else } failure
\end{array}
$$

Using sat and appropriate predicates from the standard prelude, we can define parsers for single digits, lower-case letters, upper-case letters, arbitrary letters, alphanumeric characters, and specific characters:

$$
\begin{array}{lll}
digit & :: & Parser\ Char \\
digit & = & sat\ isDigit \\
lower & :: & Parser\ Char \\
lower & = & sat\ isLower \\
upper & :: & Parser\ Char \\
upper & = & sat\ isUpper \\
letter & :: & Parser\ Char \\
letter & = & sat\ isAlpha \\
alphanum & :: & Parser\ Char \\
alphanum & = & sat\ isAlphaNum \\
char & :: & Char \rightarrow Parser\ Char \\
char\ x & = & sat\ (== x)
\end{array}
$$

For example:

```
> parse digit "123"
[('1',"23")]

> parse digit "abc"
[]

> parse (char 'a') "abc"
[('a',"bc")]

> parse (char 'a') "123"
[]
```

In turn, using *char* we can define a parser *string xs* for the string of characters *xs*, with the string itself returned as the result value:

$$
\begin{array}{lll}
string & :: & String \rightarrow Parser\ String \\
string\ [\,] & = & return\ [\,] \\
string\ (x:xs) & = & \textbf{do}\ char\ x \\
& & \quad\ string\ xs \\
& & \quad\ return\ (x:xs)
\end{array}
$$

Note that *string* is defined using recursion, and only succeeds if the entire target string is consumed. The base case states that the empty string can always be parsed. The recursive case states that a non-empty string can be parsed by parsing the first character, parsing the remaining characters, and returning the entire string as the result value. For example:

```
> parse (string "abc") "abcdef"
[("abc","def")]

> parse (string "abc") "ab1234"
[]
```

Our next two parsers, *many p* and *many1 p*, apply a parser *p* as many times as possible until it fails, with the result values from each successful application of *p* being combined as a list. The difference between these two repetition primitives is that *many* permits zero or more applications of *p*, whereas *many1* requires at least one successful application:

$$
\begin{aligned}
many & \quad :: \quad Parser\ a \rightarrow Parser\ [a] \\
many\ p & \quad = \quad many1\ p \mathbin{+\!\!+\!\!+} return\ [\,] \\[4pt]
many1 & \quad :: \quad Parser\ a \rightarrow Parser\ [a] \\
many1\ p & \quad = \quad \textbf{do}\ v \leftarrow p \\
& \qquad\qquad vs \leftarrow many\ p \\
& \qquad\qquad return\ (v : vs)
\end{aligned}
$$

Note that *many* and *many1* are defined using mutual recursion. In particular, the definition for *many p* states that *p* can either be applied at least once or not at all, while the definition for *many1 p* states that *p* can be applied once and then zero or more times. For example:

```
> parse (many digit) "123abc"
[("123", "abc")]

> parse (many digit) "abcdef"
[("", "abcdef")]

> parse (many1 digit) "abcdef"
[]
```

Using *many* and *many1*, we can define parsers for *identifiers* (variable names) comprising a lower-case letter followed by zero or more alphanumeric characters, natural numbers comprising one or more digits, and spacing comprising zero or more space, tab, and newline characters:

$$
\begin{aligned}
ident & \quad :: \quad Parser\ String \\
ident & \quad = \quad \textbf{do}\ x \leftarrow lower \\
& \qquad\qquad xs \leftarrow many\ alphanum \\
& \qquad\qquad return\ (x : xs) \\[4pt]
nat & \quad :: \quad Parser\ Int \\
nat & \quad = \quad \textbf{do}\ xs \leftarrow many1\ digit \\
& \qquad\qquad return\ (read\ xs) \\[4pt]
space & \quad :: \quad Parser\ () \\
space & \quad = \quad \textbf{do}\ many\ (sat\ isSpace) \\
& \qquad\qquad return\ ()
\end{aligned}
$$

For example:

```
> parse ident "abc def"
[("abc", " def")]

> parse nat "123 abc"
[(123, " abc")]

> parse space "   abc"
[((), "abc")]
```

Note that *space* returns the empty tuple () as a dummy result value, reflecting the fact that the details of spacing are not usually important.

8.7 | Handling spacing

Most real-life parsers allow spacing to be freely used around the basic *tokens* in their input string. For example, the strings 1+2 and 1 + 2 are both parsed in the same way by Hugs. To handle such spacing, we define a new primitive that ignores any space before and after applying a parser for a token:

$$
\begin{aligned}
&token \quad :: \quad Parser\ a \rightarrow Parser\ a \\
&token\ p \quad = \quad \textbf{do}\ space \\
&\qquad\qquad\qquad\quad v \leftarrow p \\
&\qquad\qquad\qquad\quad space \\
&\qquad\qquad\qquad\quad return\ v
\end{aligned}
$$

Using *token*, it is now easy to define parsers that ignore spacing around identifiers, natural numbers, and special symbols:

$$
\begin{aligned}
&identifier \quad :: \quad Parser\ String \\
&identifier \quad = \quad token\ ident \\[4pt]
&natural \quad :: \quad Parser\ Int \\
&natural \quad = \quad token\ nat \\[4pt]
&symbol \quad :: \quad String \rightarrow Parser\ String \\
&symbol\ xs \quad = \quad token\ (string\ xs)
\end{aligned}
$$

For example, a parser for a non-empty list of natural numbers that ignores spacing around tokens can be defined as follows:

$$
\begin{aligned}
&p \quad :: \quad Parser\ [Int] \\
&p \quad = \quad \textbf{do}\ symbol\ "[" \\
&\qquad\qquad\quad n \leftarrow natural \\
&\qquad\qquad\quad ns \leftarrow many\ (\textbf{do}\ symbol\ "," \\
&\qquad\qquad\qquad\qquad\qquad\qquad\qquad natural) \\
&\qquad\qquad\quad symbol\ "]" \\
&\qquad\qquad\quad return\ (n : ns)
\end{aligned}
$$

This definition states that such a list begins with an opening square bracket and a natural number, followed by zero or more commas and natural numbers, and concludes with a closing square bracket. Note that p only succeeds if a complete list in precisely this format is consumed:

```
> parse p "  [1, 2, 3]  "
[([1, 2, 3], "")]

> parse p "[1,2,]"
[]
```

8.8 | Arithmetic expressions

We conclude this chapter with an extended example. Consider a simple form of arithmetic expressions built up from natural numbers using addition, multiplication, and parentheses. We assume that addition and multiplication associate to the right, and that multiplication has higher priority than addition. For example, $2 + 3 + 4$ means $2 + (3 + 4)$, while $2 * 3 + 4$ means $(2 * 3) + 4$.

The syntactic structure of a language can be formalised using the mathematical notion of a *grammar*, which is a set of rules that describes how strings of the language can be constructed. For example, a grammar for our language of arithmetic expressions can be defined by the following two rules:

$$
\begin{aligned}
expr &::= & expr + expr \mid expr * expr \mid (expr) \mid nat \\
nat &::= & 0 \mid 1 \mid 2 \mid \cdots
\end{aligned}
$$

The first rule states that an expression is either the addition or multiplication of two expressions, a parenthesised expression, or a natural number. In turn, the second rule states that a natural number is either zero, one, two, etc. For example, using this grammar the construction of the expression $2 * 3 + 4$ can be represented by the following *parse tree*, in which the tokens in the expression appear at the leaves, and the grammatical rules applied to construct the expression give rise to the branching structure:

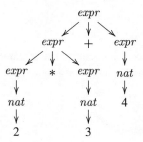

The structure of this tree makes explicit that $2 * 3 + 4$ can be constructed from the addition of two expressions, the first given by the multiplication of two further expressions which are in turn given by the numbers two and three, and the second expression given by the number four. However, the grammar also permits another possible parse tree for this example, which corresponds to the erroneous interpretation of the expression as $2 * (3 + 4)$:

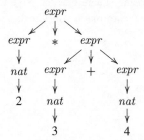

The problem is that our grammar for expressions does not take account of the fact that multiplication has higher priority than addition. However, this can easily be fixed by modifying the grammar to have a separate rule for each level of priority, with addition at the lowest level of priority, multiplication at the middle level, and parentheses and numbers at the highest level:

$$
\begin{aligned}
expr &\ ::=\ expr + expr \mid term \\
term &\ ::=\ term * term \mid factor \\
factor &\ ::=\ (expr) \mid nat \\
nat &\ ::=\ 0 \mid 1 \mid 2 \mid \cdots
\end{aligned}
$$

Using this new grammar, $2 * 3 + 4$ indeed has a single parse tree, which corresponds to the correct interpretation of the expression as $(2 * 3) + 4$:

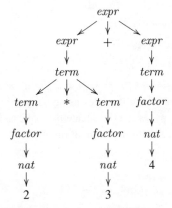

We have now dealt with the issue of priority, but our grammar does not yet take account of the fact that addition and multiplication associate to the right. For example, the expression $2 + 3 + 4$ currently has two possible parse trees, corresponding to $(2 + 3) + 4$ and $2 + (3 + 4)$. However, this can also easily be fixed by modifying the grammatical rules for addition and multiplication to be recursive in their right argument only, rather than both arguments:

$$
\begin{aligned}
expr &\ ::=\ term + expr \mid term \\
term &\ ::=\ factor * term \mid factor
\end{aligned}
$$

Using these new rules, $2 + 3 + 4$ now has a single parse tree, which corresponds to the correct interpretation of the expression as $2 + (3 + 4)$:

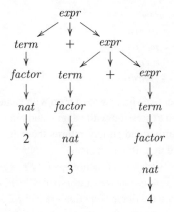

In fact, our grammar for expressions is now unambiguous, in the sense that every well-formed expression has precisely one parse tree.

Our final modification to the grammar is one of simplification. For example, consider the rule $expr ::= term + expr \mid term$, which states that an expression is either the addition of a term and an expression, or is a term. In other words, an expression always begins with a term, which can then be followed by the addition of an expression or by nothing. Hence, the rule for expressions can be simplified to $expr ::= term \, (+ \, expr \mid \epsilon)$, in which the symbol ϵ denotes the empty string. Simplifying the rule for terms in a similar manner gives our final grammar for arithmetic expressions:

$$
\begin{array}{lcl}
expr & ::= & term \, (+ \, expr \mid \epsilon) \\
term & ::= & factor \, (* \, term \mid \epsilon) \\
factor & ::= & (expr) \mid nat \\
nat & ::= & 0 \mid 1 \mid 2 \mid \cdots
\end{array}
$$

It is now straightforward to translate this grammar into a parser for expressions, by simply rewriting the rules using our parsing primitives. In fact, we choose to have the parser itself evaluate the expression being parsed to its integer value, rather than returning some form of tree:

$$
\begin{array}{lcl}
expr & :: & Parser \; Int \\
expr & = & \textbf{do} \; t \leftarrow term \\
& & \quad \textbf{do} \; symbol \; "+" \\
& & \qquad e \leftarrow expr \\
& & \qquad return \; (t + e) \\
& & \quad {+\!+\!+} \; return \; t
\end{array}
$$

$$
\begin{array}{lcl}
term & :: & Parser \; Int \\
term & = & \textbf{do} \; f \leftarrow factor \\
& & \quad \textbf{do} \; symbol \; "*" \\
& & \qquad t \leftarrow term \\
& & \qquad return \; (f * t) \\
& & \quad {+\!+\!+} \; return \; f
\end{array}
$$

$$
\begin{array}{lcl}
factor & :: & Parser \; Int \\
factor & = & \textbf{do} \; symbol \; "(" \\
& & \qquad e \leftarrow expr \\
& & \qquad symbol \; ")" \\
& & \qquad return \; e \\
& & \quad {+\!+\!+} \; natural
\end{array}
$$

For example, the parser $expr$ first parses a term with value t, then parses a plus symbol followed by an expression with value e and returns the value $t + e$, or else parses nothing further and simply returns the value t. The parsers $term$ and $factor$ can be read in a similar manner.

Finally, using $expr$ we define a function $eval :: String \to Int$ that evaluates an arithmetic expression to its integer value. To handle the cases of unconsumed and invalid input, we use the library function $error :: String \to a$ that displays an error message and then terminates the program:

$$eval \quad :: \quad String \to Int$$

$eval\ xs\ =\ $**case** $parse\ expr\ xs$ **of**

$\qquad\qquad [(n, [\,])] \to n$

$\qquad\qquad [(\_, out)] \to error\,(\texttt{"unused input "} \mathbin{+\!\!+} out)$

$\qquad\qquad [\,] \to error\ \texttt{"invalid input"}$

For example:

> $eval$ `"2*3+4"`
10

> $eval$ `"2*(3+4)"`
14

> $eval$ `"2 * (3 + 4)"`
14

> $eval$ `"2*3-4"`
$Error: unused\ input - 4$

> $eval$ `"-1"`
$Error: invalid\ input$

8.9 | Chapter remarks

A library file comprising the parsing primitives from this chapter is available from the book's website. For technical reasons concerning the monadic nature of parsers, a number of the basic definitions in this library are slightly different to those given here. Further details are available in (16; 17), upon which this chapter is based. More information concerning grammars can be found in (27), and more advanced approaches to building parsers in Haskell are given in (22; 9). The reading of the parser type as a rhyme is due to Fritz Ruehr.

8.10 | Exercises

1. The library file also defines a parser $int :: Parser\ Int$ for an integer. Without looking at this definition, define int. Hint: an integer is either a minus symbol followed by a natural number, or a natural number.

2. Define a parser $comment :: Parser\ ()$ for ordinary Haskell comments that begin with the symbol -- and extend to the end of the current line, which is represented by the control character `'\n'`.

3. Using our second grammar for arithmetic expressions, draw the two possible parse trees for the expression $2 + 3 + 4$.

4. Using our third grammar for arithmetic expressions, draw the parse trees for the expressions $2 + 3$, $2 * 3 * 4$ and $(2 + 3) + 4$.

5. Explain why the final simplification of the grammar for arithmetic expressions has a dramatic effect on the efficiency of the resulting parser. Hint: begin by considering how an expression comprising a single number would be parsed if this step had not been made.

6. Extend the parser for arithmetic expressions to support subtraction and division, based upon the following extensions to the grammar:

$$expr \quad ::= \quad term \; (+ \; expr \mid - \; expr \mid \epsilon)$$
$$term \quad ::= \quad factor \; (* \; term \mid / \; term \mid \epsilon)$$

7. Further extend the grammar and parser for arithmetic expressions to support exponentiation, which is assumed to associate to the right and have higher priority than multiplication and division, but lower priority than parentheses and numbers. For example, $2 \uparrow 3 * 4$ means $(2 \uparrow 3) * 4$. Hint: the new level of priority requires a new rule in the grammar.

8. Consider expressions built up from natural numbers using a subtraction operator that is assumed to associate to the left.

   (a) Define a natural grammar for such expressions.
   (b) Translate this grammar into a parser $expr :: Parser\ Int$.
   (c) What is the problem with this parser?
   (d) Show how it can be fixed. Hint: rewrite the parser using the repetition primitive $many$ and the library function $foldl$.

chapter 9

Interactive programs

In this chapter we show how Haskell can be used to write interactive programs. We start by explaining what interactive programs are, show how such programs can naturally be viewed as functions, define a number of basic interactive programs and higher-order functions for combining interactive programs, and conclude by developing a calculator and the game of life.

9.1 | Interaction

A *batch* program is one that does not interact with the user while it is running. In the early days of computing, most programs were batch programs, run in isolation from their users in order to maximise the amount of time that the computer was performing useful work. For example, a route-planning program may take start and finish points as its input, silently perform a large number of calculations, and then produce a recommended route as its output.

Up to this point in the book we have considered how Haskell can be used to write batch programs. In Haskell such programs, and more generally all programs, are modelled as *pure* functions that take all their input as explicit arguments, and produce all their output as explicit results. For example, a route planner may be modelled as a function of type $(Point, Point) \rightarrow Route$ that takes a pair of points and produces a route between them.

In contrast, an *interactive* program is one that may take additional input from the user, and produce additional output for the user, while the program is running. In the modern era of computing, most programs are interactive programs, run as a dialogue with their users in order to provide increased flexibility. For example, a calculator program may allow the user to enter numeric expressions interactively using the keyboard, and immediately display the value of such expressions on the screen.

At first sight, modelling interactive programs as pure functions may seem infeasible, because such programs by their very nature require the *side effects* of taking additional input and producing additional output while the program is running. For example, how can the calculator program described above be viewed as a pure function from arguments to results?

Over the years there have been many proposed solutions to the problem of combining the notion of pure functions with that of side effects. In the remainder of this chapter we present the solution that is adopted in Haskell, which is based upon the use of a new type in conjunction with a small number of primitives. As we shall see, this approach shares much in common with the approach to parsers presented in the previous chapter.

9.2 | The input/output type

In Haskell, an interactive program is viewed as a pure function that takes the current "state of the world" as its argument, and produces a modified world as its result, in which the modified world reflects any side effects performed by the program. Hence, given a suitable type $World$ whose values represent the current state of the world, the notion of an interactive program can be represented by a function of type $World \rightarrow World$, which we abbreviate as IO (short for "input/output") as follows:

$$\textbf{type } IO \ = \ World \rightarrow World$$

In general, however, an interactive program may return a result value in addition to performing side effects. For example, a program for reading a character from the keyboard may return the character that was read. For this reason, we generalise our type for interactive programs to also return a result value, with the type of such values being a parameter of the IO type:

$$\textbf{type } IO \ a \ = \ World \rightarrow (a, World)$$

Expressions of type $IO \ a$ are called *actions*. For example, $IO \ Char$ is the type of actions that return a character, while $IO \ ()$ is the type of actions that return the empty tuple () as a dummy result value. Actions of the latter type can be thought of as purely side-effecting actions that return no result value, and are frequently used when writing interactive programs.

In addition to returning a result value, interactive programs may also require argument values. However, there is no need to generalise the type of actions to take account of this, because this behaviour can already be achieved by exploiting currying. For example, an interactive program that takes a character and returns an integer would have type $Char \rightarrow IO \ Int$, which abbreviates the curried function type $Char \rightarrow World \rightarrow (Int, World)$.

At this point the reader may, quite understandably, be concerned about the feasibility of passing around the entire state of the world when programming with actions. In reality, Haskell systems such as Hugs implement actions in a more efficient manner than described above, but, for the purposes of understanding the behaviour of actions, this abstract view will suffice.

9.3 | Basic actions

We now introduce three basic actions for building interactive programs. First of all, the action $getChar$ reads a character from the keyboard, echoes it to the screen, and returns the character as its result value:

$$getChar \quad :: \quad IO \ Char$$
$$getChar \quad = \quad \cdots$$

The actual definition for *getChar* is built-in to the Hugs system, and cannot be defined within Haskell itself. If there are no characters waiting to be read from the keyboard, *getChar* waits until one is typed.

The dual action, *putChar c*, writes the character c to the screen, and returns no result value, represented by the empty tuple:

$$putChar \quad :: \quad Char \rightarrow IO \ ()$$
$$putChar \ c \quad = \quad \cdots$$

Our final basic action is *return v*, which simply returns the result value v without performing any interaction:

$$return \quad :: \quad a \rightarrow IO \ a$$
$$return \ v \quad = \quad \lambda world \rightarrow (v, world)$$

The function *return* provides a bridge from the setting of pure expressions without side effects to that of impure actions with side effects. Crucially, however, there is no bridge back — once we are impure we are impure for ever, with no possibility for redemption! As a result, we may suspect that impurity quickly permeates entire programs, but in practice this is usually not the case. For most Haskell programs, the vast majority of functions do not involve interaction, with this being handled by a relatively small number of interactive functions at the outermost level.

We conclude this section by noting that evaluating an action using Hugs performs its side effects, and discards the resulting value. For example, evaluating *putChar* 'a' writes the character 'a' to the screen, discards the result value from this action, and then terminates:

```
> putChar 'a'
'a'
```

9.4 | Sequencing

As with parsers, the natural way of combining two actions is to perform one after the other in sequence, with the modified world returned by the first action becoming the current world for the second, by means of a sequencing operator $\ggg$ (read as "then") defined as follows:

$$(\ggg) \quad :: \quad IO \ a \rightarrow (a \rightarrow IO \ b) \rightarrow IO \ b$$
$$f \ggg g \quad = \quad \lambda world \rightarrow \textbf{case} \ f \ world \ \textbf{of}$$
$$(v, world') \rightarrow g \ v \ world'$$

That is, we apply the action f to the current world, then apply the function g to the result value to give a second action, which is then applied to the modified world to give the final result. In practice, however, as with parsers in the previous chapter, the **do** notation is normally used to express actions defined using $\ggg$ in a more appealing form.

For example, using the **do** notation the primitive *getChar* could be decomposed into the actions of reading a character from the keyboard, echoing it to the screen, and returning the character as the result:

$$getChar \quad :: \quad IO\ Char$$
$$getChar \quad = \quad \textbf{do}\ x \leftarrow getCh$$
$$putChar\ x$$
$$return\ x$$

The action *getCh* that reads a character without echoing is not part of the standard prelude, but is provided as an extension by Hugs and can be made available in any script by including the following special line:

$$primitive\ getCh :: IO\ Char$$

9.5 | Derived primitives

Using the three basic actions together with sequencing, we can now define a number of other useful action primitives. First of all, we define an action *getLine* that reads a string of characters from the keyboard:

$$getLine \quad :: \quad IO\ String$$
$$getLine \quad = \quad \textbf{do}\ x \leftarrow getChar$$
$$\textbf{if}\ x == '\backslash n'\ \textbf{then}$$
$$return\ [\,]$$
$$\textbf{else}$$
$$\textbf{do}\ xs \leftarrow getLine$$
$$return\ (x : xs)$$

(The symbol $'\backslash n'$ represents a newline character.) Dually, we define actions *putStr* and *putStrLn* that write a string to the screen, with the latter action also moving on to a new line afterwards:

$$putStr \qquad\qquad :: \quad String \rightarrow IO\ ()$$
$$putStr\ [\,] \qquad\quad = \quad return\ ()$$
$$putStr\ (x : xs) \quad = \quad \textbf{do}\ putChar\ x$$
$$putStr\ xs$$

$$putStrLn \qquad\quad :: \quad String \rightarrow IO\ ()$$
$$putStrLn\ xs \quad\quad = \quad \textbf{do}\ putStr\ xs$$
$$putChar\ '\backslash n'$$

For example, using these primitives we can now define an action that prompts for a string to be entered from the keyboard, and then displays its length:

$$strlen \quad :: \quad IO\ ()$$
$$strlen \quad = \quad \textbf{do}\ putStr\ \texttt{"Enter a string: "}$$
$$xs \leftarrow getLine$$
$$putStr\ \texttt{"The string has "}$$
$$putStr\ (show\ (length\ xs))$$
$$putStrLn\ \texttt{" characters"}$$

For example:

> *strlen*
> *Enter a string* : *abcde*
> *The string has* 5 *characters*

In addition to the library primitives defined above, for the purposes of examples in the remainder of this chapter it is also useful to define a number of other primitives. First of all, we define actions that sound a beep and clear the screen, by displaying the appropriate control characters:

beep :: *IO* ()
beep = *putStr* "\BEL"

cls :: *IO* ()
cls = *putStr* "\ESC[2J"

By convention, the position of each character on the screen is given by a pair (x, y) of positive integers, with $(1, 1)$ being the top-left corner. The notion of such a position can be represented by the following type:

type *Pos* = (*Int*, *Int*)

Using the appropriate control characters, we can now define a function that moves the cursor to a given position, where the cursor is a marker that indicates where the next character displayed will appear:

goto :: *Pos* → *IO* ()
goto (x, y) =
    putStr ("\ESC[" ++ *show y* ++ ";" ++ *show x* ++ "H")

In turn, we define a function that displays a string at a given position:

writeat :: *Pos* → *String* → *IO* ()
writeat p xs = **do** *goto p*
                putStr xs

Finally, we define a function *seqn* that performs a list of actions in sequence, discarding their result values and returning no result:

seqn :: [*IO a*] → *IO* ()
seqn [ ] = *return* ()
seqn (*a* : *as*) = **do** *a*
                seqn as

For example, using *seqn* and a list comprehension, the above definition for *putStr* can be rewritten more compactly as follows:

putStr xs = *seqn* [*putChar x* | *x* ← *xs*]

9.6 | Calculator

At the end of the previous chapter we developed a parser for arithmetic expressions. We now extend this example to produce a simple calculator, which allows the user to enter arithmetic expressions interactively using the keyboard, and displays the value of such expressions on the screen.

Our calculator will handle expressions built up from integers using addition, subtraction, multiplication, division, and parentheses. As the subject of this chapter is interactive programs, we do not concern ourselves with the details of parsing and evaluating expressions, assuming that we are given a suitable parser *expr* :: *Parser Int* for this purpose. Such a parser can be obtained by solving some of the exercises from the previous chapter.

We begin by considering the user interface of the calculator. First of all, we define the box of the calculator as a list of strings:

```
box  ::  [String]
box  =   ["+---------------+",
         "|               |",
         "+---+---+---+---+",
         "| q | c | d | = |",
         "+---+---+---+---+",
         "| 1 | 2 | 3 | + |",
         "+---+---+---+---+",
         "| 4 | 5 | 6 | - |",
         "+---+---+---+---+",
         "| 7 | 8 | 9 | * |",
         "+---+---+---+---+",
         "| 0 | ( | ) | / |",
         "+---+---+---+---+"]
```

The first four buttons on the calculator, q, c, d, and =, allow the user to quit, clear the display, delete a character, and evaluate an expression, while the remaining sixteen buttons allow the user to enter expressions.

We also define the buttons on the calculator as a list of characters, comprising both the twenty standard buttons that appear on the box itself, together with a number of extra characters that will be allowed for flexibility, namely Q, C, D, space, escape, backspace, delete, and newline:

```
buttons  ::  [Char]
buttons  =   standard ++ extra
             where
                standard = "qcd=123+456-789*0()/"
                extra = "QCD \ESC\BS\DEL\n"
```

Using a list comprehension, we can define an action that displays the calculator box in the top-left corner of the screen:

```
showbox  ::  IO ()
showbox  =   seqn [writeat (1, y) xs | (y, xs) ← zip [1..13] box]
```

The last part of the user interface is to define a function that shows a string in the display of the calculator, by first clearing the display and then showing the last thirteen characters of the string. In this manner, if the user deletes characters from the string, they will automatically be removed from the display, and if the user types more than thirteen characters, the display will appear to scroll to the left as additional characters are typed.

$$display \quad :: \quad String \rightarrow IO\;()$$
$$display\;xs \quad = \quad \mathbf{do}\;writeat\;(3, 2)\;"\qquad\qquad\qquad "$$
$$writeat\;(3, 2)\;(reverse\;(take\;13\;(reverse\;xs)))$$

The calculator itself is controlled by a function *calc* that displays the current string, and then reads a character from the keyboard without echoing it. If this character is a valid button, then it is processed, otherwise we sound a beep to indicate an error and continue with the same string:

$$calc \quad :: \quad String \rightarrow IO\;()$$
$$calc\;xs \quad = \quad \mathbf{do}\;display\;xs$$
$$c \leftarrow getCh$$
$$\mathbf{if}\;elem\;c\;buttons\;\mathbf{then}$$
$$process\;c\;xs$$
$$\mathbf{else}$$
$$\mathbf{do}\;beep$$
$$calc\;xs$$

The function *process* takes a valid character and the current string, and performs the appropriate action depending upon the character:

$$process \qquad\qquad\qquad :: \quad Char \rightarrow String \rightarrow IO\;()$$
$$process\;c\;xs$$
$$\mid elem\;c\;"qQ\backslash ESC" \quad = \quad quit$$
$$\mid elem\;c\;"dD\backslash BS\backslash DEL" \quad = \quad delete\;xs$$
$$\mid elem\;c\;"=\backslash n" \quad = \quad eval\;xs$$
$$\mid elem\;c\;"cC" \quad = \quad clear$$
$$\mid otherwise \quad = \quad press\;c\;xs$$

We now consider each of the five possible actions in turn.

- Quitting moves the cursor below the calculator box and terminates:

$$quit \quad :: \quad IO\;()$$
$$quit \quad = \quad goto\;(1, 14)$$

- Deleting has no effect if the current string is empty, and otherwise removes the last character from this string:

$$delete \quad :: \quad String \rightarrow IO\;()$$
$$delete\;"" \quad = \quad calc\;""$$
$$delete\;xs \quad = \quad calc\;(init\;xs)$$

- Evaluation displays the result of parsing and evaluating the current string, sounding a beep if this process is unsuccessful:

$$eval \quad :: \quad String \rightarrow IO\;()$$
$$eval\;xs \quad = \quad \mathbf{case}\;parse\;expr\;xs\;\mathbf{of}$$
$$[(n, "")] \rightarrow calc\;(show\;n)$$
$$\_ \rightarrow \mathbf{do}\;beep$$
$$calc\;xs$$

- Clearing the display resets the current string to empty:

$$clear \ :: \ IO\,()$$
$$clear \ = \ calc\,"\,"$$

- Any other character is appended to the end of the current string:

$$press \ :: \ Char \to String \to IO\,()$$
$$press\ c\ xs \ = \ calc\,(xs \mathbin{+\!\!+} [\,c\,])$$

Finally, we define a function that runs the calculator, by clearing the screen, displaying the box, and starting with an empty display:

$$run \ :: \ IO\,()$$
$$run \ = \ \textbf{do}\ cls$$
$$\qquad\qquad showbox$$
$$\qquad\qquad clear$$

9.7 | Game of life

We conclude this chapter with a second extended example, concerning the *game of life*. The game models a simple evolutionary system, and is played on a two-dimentional board. Each square on the board is either empty, or contains a single living cell, as shown in the following example:

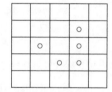

Each internal square on the board has eight immediate neighbours:

For uniformity, each square on the edge of the board is also viewed as having eight neighbours, by assuming that the board wraps around from top-to-bottom and from left-to-right. That is, we can think of the board as really being a torus, which can be viewed as the surface of a three-dimensional doughnut shaped object.

Given an initial configuration of the board, the next *generation* is given by simultaneously applying the following rules to all squares:

- a living cell survives if it has precisely two or three neighbouring squares that contain living cells, and dies (becomes empty) otherwise;

- an empty square gives birth to a living cell if it has precisely three neighbours that contain living cells, and remains empty otherwise.

For example, applying these rules to the above board gives:

By repeating this procedure with the new board, an infinite sequence of generations can be produced. By careful design of the initial configuration, many interesting patterns of behaviour can be observed in this sequence. For example, the above arrangement of cells is called a glider, and over successive generations will move diagonally down the board.

Despite its simplicity, the game of life is in fact computationally complete, in the sense that any computational process can be simulated within it by means of a suitable encoding. In the remainder of this section we show how the game of life can be implemented in Haskell.

To allow the size of the board to be easily modified, we define two integer values that determine the width and height of the board in squares:

```
width  :: Int
width  =  5

height :: Int
height =  5
```

We represent a board as a list of the (x, y) positions at which there is a living cell, using the same coordinate convention as the screen:

```
type Board  =  [Pos]
```

For example, the initial example board above would be represented by:

```
glider :: Board
glider =  [(4, 2), (2, 3), (4, 3), (3, 4), (4, 4)]
```

Using this representation of a board, it is easy to display the living cells on the screen, and to decide if a given position is alive or empty:

```
showcells   :: Board → IO ()
showcells b =  seqn [writeat p "O" | p ← b]

isAlive     :: Board → Pos → Bool
isAlive b p =  elem p b

isEmpty     :: Board → Pos → Bool
isEmpty b p =  ¬ (isAlive b p)
```

Next, we define a function that returns the neighbours of a position:

```
neighbs       :: Pos → [Pos]
neighbs (x, y) =  map wrap [(x − 1, y − 1), (x, y − 1),
                            (x + 1, y − 1), (x − 1, y),
                            (x + 1, y), (x − 1, y + 1),
                            (x, y + 1), (x + 1, y + 1)]
```

The auxiliary function *wrap* takes account of the wrapping around at the edges of the board, by subtracting one from each component of the given position, taking the remainder when divided by the width and height of the board, and then adding one to each component again:

$$
\begin{aligned}
wrap \quad & :: \quad Pos \to Pos \\
wrap\ (x, y) \quad & = \quad (((x - 1)\ `mod`\ width) + 1, \\
& \qquad ((y - 1)\ `mod`\ height) + 1)
\end{aligned}
$$

Using function composition, we can now define a function that calculates the number of live neighbours for a given position by producing the list of its neighbours, retaining those that are alive, and counting their number:

$$
\begin{aligned}
liveneighbs \quad & :: \quad Board \to Pos \to Int \\
liveneighbs\ b \quad & = \quad length \circ filter\ (isAlive\ b) \circ neighbs
\end{aligned}
$$

Using this function, it is then straightforward to produce the list of living positions in a board that have precisely two or three living neighbours, and hence survive to the next generation:

$$
\begin{aligned}
survivors \quad & :: \quad Board \to [\,Pos\,] \\
survivors\ b \quad & = \quad [\,p \mid p \leftarrow b,\ elem\ (liveneighbs\ b\ p)\ [2, 3]\,]
\end{aligned}
$$

In turn, the list of empty positions in a board that have precisely three living neighbours, and hence give birth to a new cell, can be produced as follows:

$$
\begin{aligned}
births \quad & :: \quad Board \to [\,Pos\,] \\
births\ b \quad & = \quad [(x, y) \mid x \leftarrow [1 \mathrel{..} width], \\
& \qquad y \leftarrow [1 \mathrel{..} height], \\
& \qquad isEmpty\ b\ (x, y), \\
& \qquad liveneighbs\ b\ (x, y) == 3]
\end{aligned}
$$

However, this definition considers every possible position on the board. A more refined approach, which may be more efficient for larger boards, is to only consider the neighbours of living cells on the board, because only such positions can potentially give rise to new births. Using this approach, the function *births* can be rewritten as follows:

$$
\begin{aligned}
births\ b \quad & = \quad [\,p \mid p \leftarrow rmdups\ (concat\ (map\ neighbs\ b)), \\
& \qquad isEmpty\ b\ p, \\
& \qquad liveneighbs\ b\ p == 3]
\end{aligned}
$$

The auxiliary function *rmdups* removes duplicates from a list, and is used above to ensure that each potential new cell is only considered once:

$$
\begin{aligned}
rmdups \quad & :: \quad Eq\ a \Rightarrow [\,a\,] \to [\,a\,] \\
rmdups\ [\,] \quad & = \quad [\,] \\
rmdups\ (x : xs) \quad & = \quad x : rmdups\ (filter\ (\neq x)\ xs)
\end{aligned}
$$

The next generation of a board can now be produced simply by appending the list of survivors and the list of new births:

$$
\begin{aligned}
nextgen \quad & :: \quad Board \to Board \\
nextgen\ b \quad & = \quad survivors\ b \mathbin{+\!\!+} births\ b
\end{aligned}
$$

Finally, we define a function *life* that implements the game of life itself, by clearing the screen, showing the living cells in the current board, waiting for a moment, and then continuing with the next generation:

$$
\begin{aligned}
&life \quad :: \quad Board \rightarrow IO\ () \\
&life\ b \quad = \quad \textbf{do}\ cls \\
&\qquad\qquad\qquad showcells\ b \\
&\qquad\qquad\qquad wait\ 5000 \\
&\qquad\qquad\qquad life\ (nextgen\ b)
\end{aligned}
$$

The function *wait* is used to slow down the game to a reasonable speed, and can be implemented by performing a given number of dummy actions:

$$
\begin{aligned}
&wait \quad :: \quad Int \rightarrow IO\ () \\
&wait\ n \quad = \quad seqn\ [return\ ()\ |\ \_ \leftarrow [1\mathinner{\ldotp\ldotp}n]]
\end{aligned}
$$

For fun, you may like to try out the *life* function with the *glider* example, and experiment with some patterns of your own.

9.8 | Chapter remarks

The use of the *IO* type to perform other forms of side effects, including reading and writing from files, and handling exceptional events, is discussed in the Haskell Report (25). A formal meaning for input/output and other forms of side effects is given in (24). A variety of libraries for performing graphical interaction are available from the Haskell home page, *www.haskell.org*. The game of life was invented by John Conway, and popularised by Martin Gardner in the October 1970 edition of Scientific American.

9.9 | Exercises

1. Define an action *readLine* :: *IO String* that behaves in the same way as *getLine*, except that it also permits the delete key to be used to remove characters. Hint: the delete character is ′\DEL′, and the control string for moving the cursor back one character is "\ESC[1D".

2. Modify the calculator program to indicate the approximate position of an error rather than just sounding a beep, by using the fact that the parser returns the unconsumed part of the input string.

3. On some systems the game of life may flicker, due to the entire screen being cleared each generation. Modify the game to avoid such flicker by only redisplaying positions whose status changes.

4. Produce an editor that allows the user to interactively create and modify the content of the board in the game of life.

5. Produce graphical versions of the calculator and game of life programs, using one of the graphics libraries available from *www.haskell.org*.

6. Nim is a game that is played on a board comprising five numbered rows of stars, which is initially set up as follows:

```
1 : * * * * *
2 : * * * *
3 : * * *
4 : **
5 : *
```

Two players take it in turn to remove one or more stars from the end of a single row. The winner is the player who removes the last star or stars from the board. Implement the game of nim in Haskell. Hint: represent the board as a list comprising the number of stars remaining on each row, with the initial board being [5, 4, 3, 2, 1].

chapter 10

Declaring types and classes

In this chapter we introduce mechanisms for declaring new types and classes in Haskell. We start with two approaches to declaring types, then consider recursive types, develop a tautology checker and an abstract machine, and conclude by showing how to declare classes and their instances.

10.1 | Type declarations

The simplest way of declaring a new type is to introduce a new name for an existing type, using the **type** mechanism of Haskell. For example, the following declaration from the standard library states that the type *String* is just a synonym for the type [*Char*] of lists of characters:

    type *String* = [*Char*]

As in this example, the name of a new type must begin with a capital letter. Type declarations can be nested, in the sense that one such type can be declared in terms of another. For example, in the previous chapter a type for boards was declared in terms of a type for positions:

    type *Board* = [*Pos*]
    type *Pos* = (*Int, Int*)

For technical reasons, however, type declarations cannot be recursive. For example, consider the following erroneous declaration:

    type *Tree* = (*Int,* [*Tree*])

That is, a tree is a pair comprising an integer and a list of subtrees. While this declaration is perfectly reasonable, with the empty list of subtrees forming the base case for the recursion, it is not permitted in Haskell because it is recursive. If required, recursive types can be declared using the more powerful **data** mechanism, which will be introduced shortly.

Type declarations can also be parameterised by other types. For example, in the previous two chapters we declared the following types for parsers and interactive programs in terms of a type parameter:

$$\textbf{type } Parser\ a \ = \ String \rightarrow [(a,\ String)]$$
$$\textbf{type } IO\ a \ \quad = \ World \rightarrow (a,\ World)$$

Declarations with more than one type parameter are also permitted. For example, a type of lookup tables that associate keys of one type to values of another type can be declared as a list of (key, value) pairs:

$$\textbf{type } Assoc\ k\ v \ = \ [(k,\ v)]$$

Using this type, a function that returns the first value that is associated with a given key in a table can then be defined as follows:

$$find \quad :: \quad Eq\ k \Rightarrow k \rightarrow Assoc\ k\ v \rightarrow v$$
$$find\ k\ t \ = \ head\ [\,v \mid (k',\ v) \leftarrow t,\ k == k'\,]$$

10.2 | Data declarations

A completely new type, as opposed to a synonym for an existing type, can be declared by specifying its values using the **data** mechanism of Haskell. For example, the following declaration from the standard library states that the type *Bool* comprises two new values, named *False* and *True*:

$$\textbf{data } Bool \ = \ False \mid True$$

In such declarations, the symbol | is read as "or", and the new values of the type are called *constructors*. As with new types themselves, the names of new constructors must begin with a capital letter. Moreover, the same constructor name cannot be used in more than one type.

Note that the names given to new types and constructors have no inherent meaning to the Hugs system. For example, the above declaration could equally well be written as **data** $A = B \mid C$, because the precise details of the names are not relevant, other than the fact that they have not been used before. The meaning of names such as *Bool*, *False*, and *True* is assigned by the programmer, via the functions that they define on new types.

Values of new types can be used in precisely the same way as those of built-in types. In particular, they can freely be passed as arguments to functions, returned as results from functions, stored in data structures such as lists, and used in patterns. For example, given the declaration

$$\textbf{data } Move \ = \ Left \mid Right \mid Up \mid Down$$

functions that apply a move to a position (recalling that positions are relative to the top-left corner of the screen), apply a list of moves to a position, and flip the direction of a move, can be defined as follows:

$$
\begin{aligned}
move &:: \ Move \to Pos \to Pos \\
move \ Left \ (x, y) &= \ (x - 1, y) \\
move \ Right \ (x, y) &= \ (x + 1, y) \\
move \ Up \ (x, y) &= \ (x, y - 1) \\
move \ Down \ (x, y) &= \ (x, y + 1) \\
\\
moves &:: \ [Move] \to Pos \to Pos \\
moves \ [\,] \ p &= \ p \\
moves \ (m : ms) \ p &= \ moves \ ms \ (move \ m \ p) \\
\\
flip &:: \ Move \to Move \\
flip \ Left &= \ Right \\
flip \ Right &= \ Left \\
flip \ Up &= \ Down \\
flip \ Down &= \ Up
\end{aligned}
$$

The constructors in a data declaration can also have arguments. For example, a type of shapes that comprise circles with a given radius, and rectangles with given dimensions can be declared by:

data $Shape \ = \ Circle \ Float \mid Rect \ Float \ Float$

That is, the type $Shape$ has values of the form $Circle \ r$, where r is a floating-point number, and $Rect \ x \ y$, where x and y are floating-point numbers. These constructors can then be used to define functions on shapes, such as to produce a square of a given size, and to calculate the area of a shape:

$$
\begin{aligned}
square &:: \ Float \to Shape \\
square \ n &= \ Rect \ n \ n \\
\\
area &:: \ Shape \to Float \\
area \ (Circle \ r) &= \ pi * r \uparrow 2 \\
area \ (Rect \ x \ y) &= \ x * y
\end{aligned}
$$

Because of their use of arguments, the constructors $Circle$ and $Rect$ are actually constructor functions, which produce results of type $Shape$ from arguments of type $Float$, as can be demonstrated using Hugs:

$$
\begin{aligned}
&> \ :type \ Circle \\
&Circle :: Float \to Shape
\end{aligned}
$$

$$
\begin{aligned}
&> \ :type \ Rect \\
&Rect :: Float \to Float \to Shape
\end{aligned}
$$

The difference between normal functions and constructor functions is that the latter have no defining equations, and exist solely for the purpose of building pieces of data. For example, whereas the expression $negate \ 1.0$ can be evaluated to -1.0 by applying the definition of $negate$, the expression $Circle \ 1.0$ is already fully evaluated, and hence cannot be further simplified, because there are no defining equations for $Circle$. Rather, the expression $Circle \ 1.0$ is just a piece of data, in the same way that 1.0 itself is just data.

Not surprisingly, data declarations themselves can also be parameterised. For example, the standard library declares the following type:

data $Maybe \ a \ = \ Nothing \mid Just \ a$

That is, a value of type *Maybe a* is either *Nothing*, or of the form *Just x* for some value *x* of type *a*. We can think of values of type *Maybe a* as being values of type *a* that may fail, with *Nothing* representing failure, and *Just* representing success. For example, using this type we can define safe versions of the library functions *div* and *head*, which return *Nothing* in the case of invalid arguments, rather than producing an error:

$$
\begin{array}{lll}
safediv & :: & Int \rightarrow Int \rightarrow Maybe\ Int \\
safediv\ \_\ 0 & = & Nothing \\
safediv\ m\ n & = & Just\ (m\ \text{`}div\text{`}\ n) \\
\\
safehead & :: & [\,a\,] \rightarrow Maybe\ a \\
safehead\ [\,] & = & Nothing \\
safehead\ xs & = & Just\ (head\ xs)
\end{array}
$$

10.3 | Recursive types

Types declared using the data mechanism can also be recursive. By way of a simple first example, consider the following recursive type:

data *Nat* = *Zero* | *Succ Nat*

That is, a value of type *Nat* is either *Zero*, or of the form *Succ n* for some value *n* of type *Nat*. Hence, this declaration gives rise to an infinite sequence of values, starting with the value *Zero*, and continuing by applying the constructor function *Succ* to the previous value in the sequence:

$$
\begin{array}{l}
Zero \\
Succ\ Zero \\
Succ\ (Succ\ Zero) \\
Succ\ (Succ\ (Succ\ Zero)) \\
\vdots
\end{array}
$$

As suggested by the choice of names, values of type *Nat* can be thought of as natural numbers (non-negative integers), with *Zero* representing the natural number 0 and *Succ* representing the successor function 1+ on such numbers. For example, *Succ (Succ (Succ Zero))* represents $1 + (1 + (1 + 0)) = 3$. More formally, we can define the following conversion functions:

$$
\begin{array}{lll}
nat2int & :: & Nat \rightarrow Int \\
nat2int\ Zero & = & 0 \\
nat2int\ (Succ\ n) & = & 1 + nat2int\ n \\
\\
int2nat & :: & Int \rightarrow Nat \\
int2nat\ 0 & = & Zero \\
int2nat\ (n+1) & = & Succ\ (int2nat\ n)
\end{array}
$$

For example, using these functions, two natural numbers can be added together by first converting them into integers, adding these integers, and then converting the result back into a natural number:

$$add \quad :: \quad Nat \rightarrow Nat \rightarrow Nat$$
$$add\ m\ n \ = \ int2nat\ (nat2int\ m + nat2int\ n)$$

However, using recursion the function add can be redefined without the need for such conversions, and hence more efficiently:

$$add\ Zero\ n \qquad = \quad n$$
$$add\ (Succ\ m)\ n \ = \quad Succ\ (add\ m\ n)$$

This definition formalises the idea that two natural numbers can be added by copying $Succ$ constructors from the first number until they are exhausted, at which point the $Zero$ at the end is replaced by the second number. For example, showing that $2 + 1 = 3$ proceeds as follows:

$$add\ (Succ\ (Succ\ Zero))\ (Succ\ Zero)$$
$$= \qquad \{\ \text{applying}\ add\ \}$$
$$Succ\ (add\ (Succ\ Zero)\ (Succ\ Zero))$$
$$= \qquad \{\ \text{applying}\ add\ \}$$
$$Succ\ (Succ\ (add\ Zero\ (Succ\ Zero)))$$
$$= \qquad \{\ \text{applying}\ add\ \}$$
$$Succ\ (Succ\ (Succ\ Zero))$$

As another example, the data mechanism can be used to declare our own version of the built-in type of lists, parameterised by an arbitrary type:

data $List\ a \ = \ Nil\ |\ Cons\ a\ (List\ a)$

That is, a value of type $List\ a$ is either Nil, representing the empty list, or of the form $Cons\ x\ xs$ for some values $x :: a$ and $xs :: List\ a$, representing a non-empty list. Using this type, we can then also define our own versions of library functions on lists, such as to calculate the length of a list:

$$len \qquad\qquad :: \quad List\ a \rightarrow Int$$
$$len\ Nil \qquad\quad = \quad 0$$
$$len\ (Cons\ \_\ xs) \ = \ 1 + len\ xs$$

While lists are perhaps the most commonly used data structure in computing, it is often useful to store data in a two-way branching structure, or *binary tree*, as depicted in the following example:

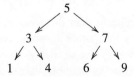

In this example, the numbers 1, 4, 6, 9 appear at the external *leaves* of the tree, and the numbers 5, 3, 7 appear at the internal *nodes*. Using recursion, a suitable type for representing such trees can be declared by:

data $Tree \ = \ Leaf\ Int\ |\ Node\ Tree\ Int\ Tree$

For simplicity, we have fixed the type of the values to integers, but this could easily be generalised by parameterising the declaration. Using this type, the tree pictured above can be represented as follows:

$$t \quad :: \quad Tree$$
$$t \quad = \quad Node\ (Node\ (Leaf\ 1)\ 3\ (Leaf\ 4))\ 5\ (Node\ (Leaf\ 6)\ 7\ (Leaf\ 9))$$

We now consider a number of functions on such trees. First of all, we define a function that decides if a given integer occurs in a tree:

$$
\begin{aligned}
occurs & \quad :: \quad Int \rightarrow Tree \rightarrow Bool \\
occurs\ m\ (Leaf\ n) & \quad = \quad m == n \\
occurs\ m\ (Node\ l\ n\ r) & \quad = \quad m == n \vee occurs\ m\ l \vee occurs\ m\ r
\end{aligned}
$$

That is, an integer occurs in a leaf if it matches the value at the leaf, and occurs in a node if it either matches the value at the node, occurs in the left subtree, or occurs in the right subtree. Note that under lazy evaluation, if either of the first two conditions in the node case is *True*, then the result *True* is returned without the need to evaluate the remaining conditions.

In the worst case, however, the function *occurs* may still traverse the entire tree, in particular when the given integer does not occur in the tree. Now consider a function that flattens a tree to a list:

$$
\begin{aligned}
flatten & \quad :: \quad Tree \rightarrow [Int] \\
flatten\ (Leaf\ n) & \quad = \quad [n] \\
flatten\ (Node\ l\ n\ r) & \quad = \quad flatten\ l \mathbin{+\!\!+} [n] \mathbin{+\!\!+} flatten\ r
\end{aligned}
$$

If applying this function results in a sorted list, then the tree itself is called a *search tree*. For instance, our example tree is a search tree, because:

$$flatten\ t \quad = \quad [1, 3, 4, 5, 6, 7, 9]$$

Search trees have the important property that, when trying to decide if a given integer occurs in a tree, which of the two subtrees of a node it may occur in can always be determined. In particular, if the integer is less than the value at the node, then it can only occur in the left subtree, and if it is greater than this value, it can only occur in the right subtree. Hence, for search trees the *occurs* function can be rewritten as follows:

$$
\begin{aligned}
occurs\ m\ (Leaf\ n) & \quad = \quad m == n \\
occurs\ m\ (Node\ l\ n\ r) & \\
\quad |\ m == n & \quad = \quad True \\
\quad |\ m < n & \quad = \quad occurs\ m\ l \\
\quad |\ otherwise & \quad = \quad occurs\ m\ r
\end{aligned}
$$

This definition is more efficient than the previous version, because it only traverses one path down the tree, rather than potentially the entire tree.

We conclude this section by noting that, as in nature, trees in computing come in many different forms. For example, we can declare types for trees that have data only in their leaves, data only in their nodes, data in both their leaves and nodes (as above), or have a list of subtrees:

$$
\begin{aligned}
\textbf{data}\ Tree\ a & \quad = \quad Leaf\ a \mid Node\ (Tree\ a)\ (Tree\ a) \\
\textbf{data}\ Tree\ a & \quad = \quad Leaf \mid Node\ (Tree\ a)\ a\ (Tree\ a) \\
\textbf{data}\ Tree\ a\ b & \quad = \quad Leaf\ a \mid Node\ (Tree\ a\ b)\ b\ (Tree\ a\ b) \\
\textbf{data}\ Tree\ a & \quad = \quad Node\ a\ [\,Tree\ a\,]
\end{aligned}
$$

Which form of tree is most appropriate depends upon the situation. Note that in the last example, there is no constructor for leaves, because a node with an empty list of subtrees can play the role of a leaf.

10.4 | Tautology checker

In practice, tree types often occur as a representation of some kind of language. In this section we present an extended example concerning such a type, by developing a function that decides if simple logical propositions are always true. Such propositions are called *tautologies*.

Consider a language of propositions built up from basic values (*False*, *True*) and variables ($A, B, \cdots, Z$) using negation ($\neg$), conjunction ($\wedge$), implication ($\Rightarrow$), and parentheses. For example, the following are all propositions:

$$A \wedge \neg A$$

$$(A \wedge B) \Rightarrow A$$

$$A \Rightarrow (A \wedge B)$$

$$(A \wedge (A \Rightarrow B)) \Rightarrow B$$

The meaning of the logical operators can be defined using *truth tables*, which give the resulting value for each combination of argument values:

A	$\neg A$
F	T
T	F

A	B	$A \wedge B$
F	F	F
F	T	F
T	F	F
T	T	T

A	B	$A \Rightarrow B$
F	F	T
F	T	T
T	F	F
T	T	T

For example, the truth table for conjunction states that $A \wedge B$ returns *True* if both A and B are *True*, and *False* otherwise. (To save space in such tables, we abbreviate the basic values by F and T.) Using these definitions, the truth table for any proposition can then be constructed. In the case of our four example propositions, the resulting tables are as follows:

A	$A \wedge \neg A$
F	F
T	F

A	B	$(A \wedge B) \Rightarrow A$
F	F	T
F	T	T
T	F	T
T	T	T

A	B	$A \Rightarrow (A \wedge B)$
F	F	T
F	T	T
T	F	F
T	T	T

A	B	$(A \wedge (A \Rightarrow B)) \Rightarrow B$
F	F	T
F	T	T
T	F	T
T	T	T

These tables show that the second and fourth propositions are tautologies, because their result value is always *True*, while the first and third are not tautologies, because their result is *False* in at least one case.

The first step towards defining a function that decides if a proposition is a tautology is to declare a type for propositions, with one constructor for each of the five possible forms that a proposition can have:

$$\begin{array}{lll}
\textbf{data } \textit{Prop} & = & \textit{Const Bool} \\
& | & \textit{Var Char} \\
& | & \textit{Not Prop} \\
& | & \textit{And Prop Prop} \\
& | & \textit{Imply Prop Prop}
\end{array}$$

Note that an explicit constructor for parentheses is not required, as parentheses within Haskell itself can be used to indicate grouping. For example, the four propositions above can be represented as follows:

$$\begin{array}{lll}
\textit{p1} & :: & \textit{Prop} \\
\textit{p1} & = & \textit{And } (\textit{Var } 'A') \, (\textit{Not } (\textit{Var } 'A')) \\
\\
\textit{p2} & :: & \textit{Prop} \\
\textit{p2} & = & \textit{Imply } (\textit{And } (\textit{Var } 'A') \, (\textit{Var } 'B')) \, (\textit{Var } 'A') \\
\\
\textit{p3} & :: & \textit{Prop} \\
\textit{p3} & = & \textit{Imply } (\textit{Var } 'A') \, (\textit{And } (\textit{Var } 'A') \, (\textit{Var } 'B')) \\
\\
\textit{p4} & :: & \textit{Prop} \\
\textit{p4} & = & \textit{Imply } (\textit{And } (\textit{Var } 'A') \, (\textit{Imply} \\
& & \quad (\textit{Var } 'A') \, (\textit{Var } 'B'))) \, (\textit{Var } 'B')
\end{array}$$

In order to evaluate a proposition to a logical value, we need to know the value of each of its variables. For this purpose, we declare a *substitution* as a lookup table that associates variable names to logical values, using the *Assoc* type that was introduced at the start of this chapter:

$$\textbf{type } \textit{Subst} \quad = \quad \textit{Assoc Char Bool}$$

For example, the substitution $[('A', \textit{False}), ('B', \textit{True})]$ assigns the variable *A* to *False*, and *B* to *True*. A function that evaluates a proposition given a substitution for its variables can now be defined by pattern matching on the five possible forms that the proposition can have:

$$\begin{array}{lll}
\textit{eval} & :: & \textit{Subst} \rightarrow \textit{Prop} \rightarrow \textit{Bool} \\
\textit{eval } \_ (\textit{Const } b) & = & b \\
\textit{eval } s \, (\textit{Var } x) & = & \textit{find } x \, s \\
\textit{eval } s \, (\textit{Not } p) & = & \neg \, (\textit{eval } s \, p) \\
\textit{eval } s \, (\textit{And } p \; q) & = & \textit{eval } s \, p \wedge \textit{eval } s \, q \\
\textit{eval } s \, (\textit{Imply } p \; q) & = & \textit{eval } s \, p \leq \textit{eval } s \, q
\end{array}$$

For example, the value of a constant proposition is simply the constant itself, the value of a variable is obtained by looking up its value in the substitution, and the value of a conjunction is given by taking the conjunction of the values of the two argument propositions. Note that logical implication $\Rightarrow$ is implemented by the $\leq$ operator on logical values.

To decide if a proposition is a tautology, we will consider all possible substitutions for the variables that it contains. First of all, we define a function that returns the variables in a proposition:

$$
\begin{array}{lll}
vars & :: & Prop \rightarrow [\,Char\,] \\
vars\ (Const\ \_) & = & [\,] \\
vars\ (Var\ x) & = & [x] \\
vars\ (Not\ p) & = & vars\ p \\
vars\ (And\ p\ q) & = & vars\ p + \!\!+ vars\ q \\
vars\ (Imply\ p\ q) & = & vars\ p + \!\!+ vars\ q
\end{array}
$$

For example, $vars\ p2 = [\,'A'\,,\,'B'\,,\,'A'\,]$. Note that this function does not remove duplicates, which will be done separately later on.

The key to generating substitutions is generating lists of logical values of a given length. To this end, we seek to define a function $bools :: Int \rightarrow [[\,Bool\,]]$ which, for example, will return all eight lists of three logical values:

```
>  bools 3
[[ False, False, False],
 [ False, False, True],
 [ False, True, False],
 [ False, True, True],
 [ True, False, False],
 [ True, False, True],
 [ True, True, False],
 [ True, True, True]]
```

The order in which the lists are produced is not important. One way to achieve this behaviour is to observe that each list corresponds to a binary number, by interpreting *False* and *True* as the binary digits 0 and 1. For example, the list [*True, False, True*] corresponds to the binary number 101. Given this interpretation, we can think of the function *bools* as simply counting in binary, starting from zero and proceeding upwards to the appropriate limit.

This idea leads to the following definition for *bools*, in terms of the function $int2bin :: Int \rightarrow [\,Bit\,]$ from chapter 7, which converts a non-negative integer into a binary number represented as a list of bits:

$$
\begin{array}{lll}
bools & :: & Int \rightarrow [[\,Bool\,]] \\
bools\ n & = & map\ (map\ conv \circ make\ n \circ int2bin)\ [0\,..\,limit] \\
& & \textbf{where} \\
& & \quad limit = (2 \uparrow n) - 1 \\
& & \quad make\ n\ bs = take\ n\ (bs + \!\!+ repeat\ 0) \\
& & \quad conv\ 0 = False \\
& & \quad conv\ 1 = True
\end{array}
$$

There is, however, a simpler way to define *bools*, which can be revealed by thinking about the structure of the resulting lists. For example, we can observe that *bools* 3 contains two copies of *bools* 2, the first preceded by *False* in each case, and the second preceded by *True* in each case:

False	*False*	*False*
False	*False*	*True*
False	*True*	*False*
False	*True*	*True*
True	*False*	*False*
True	*False*	*True*
True	*True*	*False*
True	*True*	*True*

This observation naturally leads to a recursive definition for *bools*. In the base case, *bools* 0, we return all lists of zero logical values, of which the empty list is the only one. In the recursive case, *bools* $(n + 1)$, we take two copies of the lists produced by *bools* n, place *False* in front of each list in the first copy, *True* in front of each list in the second, and append the results:

$$
\begin{array}{lll}
bools & :: & Int \rightarrow [[Bool]] \\
bools\ 0 & = & [[\,]] \\
bools\ (n+1) & = & map\ (False:)\ bss \mathbin{+\!\!+} map\ (True:)\ bss \\
& & \textbf{where}\ bss = bools\ n
\end{array}
$$

Using *bools*, it is now straightforward to define a function that generates all substitutions for a proposition by extracting its variables, removing duplicates from this list (using the function *rmdups* from chapter 9), generating all possible lists of logical values for this many variables, and then zipping the list of variables with each of the resulting lists:

$$
\begin{array}{lll}
substs & :: & Prop \rightarrow [Subst] \\
substs\ p & = & map\ (zip\ vs)\ (bools\ (length\ vs)) \\
& & \textbf{where}\ vs = rmdups\ (vars\ p)
\end{array}
$$

For example:

```
> substs p2
[[('A', False), ('B', False)],
 [('A', False), ('B', True)],
 [('A', True), ('B', False)],
 [('A', True), ('B', True)]]
```

Finally, we define a function that decides if a proposition is a tautology, by checking if it evaluates to *True* for all possible substitutions:

$$
\begin{array}{lll}
isTaut & :: & Prop \rightarrow Bool \\
isTaut\ p & = & and\ [eval\ s\ p \mid s \leftarrow substs\ p]
\end{array}
$$

For example:

```
> isTaut p1
False
```

> *isTaut p2*
True

> *isTaut p3*
False

> *isTaut p4*
True

10.5 | Abstract machine

As a second extended example, consider a type of simple arithmetic expressions built up from integers using an addition operator, together with a function that evaluates such an expression to an integer value:

$$
\begin{aligned}
&\textbf{data } Expr &&= && Val\ Int \mid Add\ Expr\ Expr \\
&value &&:: && Expr \rightarrow Int \\
&value\ (Val\ n) &&= && n \\
&value\ (Add\ x\ y) &&= && value\ x + value\ y
\end{aligned}
$$

For example, the expression $(2 + 3) + 4$ is evaluated as follows:

$$
\begin{aligned}
&\quad value\ (Add\ (Add\ (Val\ 2)\ (Val\ 3))\ (Val\ 4)) \\
&= \quad \{\text{applying } value\ \} \\
&\quad value\ (Add\ (Val\ 2)\ (Val\ 3)) + value\ (Val\ 4) \\
&= \quad \{\text{applying the first } value\ \} \\
&\quad (value\ (Val\ 2) + value\ (Val\ 3)) + value\ (Val\ 4) \\
&= \quad \{\text{applying the first } value\ \} \\
&\quad (2 + value\ (Val\ 3)) + value\ (Val\ 4) \\
&= \quad \{\text{applying the first } value\ \} \\
&\quad (2 + 3) + value\ (Val\ 4) \\
&= \quad \{\text{applying the first } +\ \} \\
&\quad 5 + value\ (Val\ 4) \\
&= \quad \{\text{applying } value\ \} \\
&\quad 5 + 4 \\
&= \quad \{\text{applying } +\ \} \\
&\quad 9
\end{aligned}
$$

Note that the definition of the *value* function does not specify that the left argument of an addition should be evaluated before the right, or, more generally, what the next step of evaluation should be at any point. Rather, the order of evaluation is determined by Haskell. If desired, however, such control information can be made explicit by defining an *abstract machine* for expressions, which specifies the step-by-step process of their evaluation.

To this end, we first declare a type of *control stacks* for the abstract machine, which comprise a list of operations to be performed by the machine after the current evaluation has been completed:

$$
\begin{aligned}
&\textbf{type } Cont &&= && [\,Op\,] \\
&\textbf{data } Op &&= && EVAL\ Expr \mid ADD\ Int
\end{aligned}
$$

The meaning of the two operations will be explained shortly. We now define a function that evaluates an expression in the context of a control stack:

$$
\begin{aligned}
&eval &&:: \quad Expr \to Cont \to Int \\
&eval\ (Val\ n)\ c &&= \quad exec\ c\ n \\
&eval\ (Add\ x\ y)\ c &&= \quad eval\ x\ (EVAL\ y : c)
\end{aligned}
$$

That is, if the expression is an integer, it is already fully evaluated, and we begin executing the control stack. If the expression is an addition, we evaluate the first argument, x, placing the operation $EVAL\ y$ on top of the control stack to indicate that the second argument, y, should be evaluated once that of the first argument is completed. In turn, we define the function that executes a control stack in the context of an integer argument:

$$
\begin{aligned}
&exec &&:: \quad Cont \to Int \to Int \\
&exec\ [\ ]\ n &&= \quad n \\
&exec\ (EVAL\ y : c)\ n &&= \quad eval\ y\ (ADD\ n : c) \\
&exec\ (ADD\ n : c)\ m &&= \quad exec\ c\ (n + m)
\end{aligned}
$$

That is, if the stack is empty, we return the integer argument as the result of the execution. If the top of the stack is an operation $EVAL\ y$, we evaluate the expression y, placing the instruction $ADD\ n$ on top of the remaining stack to indicate that the current integer argument, n, should be added together with the result of evaluating y once this is completed. And, finally, if the top of the stack is an operation $ADD\ n$, evaluation of the two arguments of an addition is now complete, and we execute the remaining control stack in the context of the sum of the two resulting integer values.

Finally, we define a function that evaluates an expression to an integer, by invoking $eval$ with the given expression and the empty control stack:

$$
\begin{aligned}
&value &&:: \quad Expr \to Int \\
&value\ e &&= \quad eval\ e\ [\ ]
\end{aligned}
$$

The fact that our abstract machine uses two mutually recursive functions, $eval$ and $exec$, reflects the fact that it has two states, depending upon whether it is being driven by the structure of the expression or the control stack. To illustrate the machine, here is how it evaluates $(2 + 3) + 4$:

$$
\begin{aligned}
&\quad value\ (Add\ (Add\ (Val\ 2)\ (Val\ 3))\ (Val\ 4)) \\
&= \quad \{\ \text{applying}\ value\ \} \\
&\quad eval\ (Add\ (Add\ (Val\ 2)\ (Val\ 3))\ (Val\ 4))\ [\ ] \\
&= \quad \{\ \text{applying}\ eval\ \} \\
&\quad eval\ (Add\ (Val\ 2)\ (Val\ 3))\ [EVAL\ (Val\ 4)] \\
&= \quad \{\ \text{applying}\ eval\ \} \\
&\quad eval\ (Val\ 2)\ [EVAL\ (Val\ 3),\ EVAL\ (Val\ 4)] \\
&= \quad \{\ \text{applying}\ eval\ \} \\
&\quad exec\ [EVAL\ (Val\ 3),\ EVAL\ (Val\ 4)]\ 2 \\
&= \quad \{\ \text{applying}\ exec\ \} \\
&\quad eval\ (Val\ 3)\ [ADD\ 2,\ EVAL\ (Val\ 4)] \\
&= \quad \{\ \text{applying}\ eval\ \} \\
&\quad exec\ [ADD\ 2,\ EVAL\ (Val\ 4)]\ 3 \\
&= \quad \{\ \text{applying}\ exec\ \}
\end{aligned}
$$

$$exec \ [EVAL \ (Val \ 4)] \ 5$$
$$= \quad \{ \text{applying } exec \}$$
$$eval \ (Val \ 4) \ [ADD \ 5]$$
$$= \quad \{ \text{applying } eval \}$$
$$exec \ [ADD \ 5] \ 4$$
$$= \quad \{ \text{applying } exec \}$$
$$exec \ [] \ 9$$
$$= \quad \{ \text{applying } exec \}$$
$$9$$

Note how *eval* proceeds downwards to the leftmost integer in the expression, maintaining a trail of the pending right-hand expressions on the control stack. In turn, *exec* then proceeds upwards through the trail, transferring control back to *eval* and performing additions as appropriate.

10.6 | Class and instance declarations

We now turn our attention from types to classes. In Haskell, a new class can be declared using the **class** mechanism. For example, the class Eq of equality types is declared in the standard library as follows:

class Eq a **where**
$$(==), (\neq) \ :: \ a \to a \to Bool$$
$$x \neq y \quad = \ \neg \ (x == y)$$

This declaration states that for a type a to be an instance of the class Eq, it must support equality and inequality operators of the specified types. In fact, because a *default definition* has already been included for $\neq$, declaring an instance of this class only requires a definition for $==$. For example, the type $Bool$ can be made into an equality type as follows:

instance Eq $Bool$ **where**
$$False == False \ = \ True$$
$$True == True \ = \ True$$
$$\_ == \_ \quad \ = \ False$$

For technical reasons, only types declared using the **data** mechanism can be made into instances of classes. Note also that default definitions can be overridden in instance declarations if desired. For example, for some equality types there may be a more efficient or appropriate way to decide if two values are different than simply checking if they are not equal.

Classes can also be extended to form new classes. For example, the class Ord of types whose values are totally ordered is declared in the standard library as an extension of the class Eq as follows:

```
class Eq a ⇒ Ord a where
   (<), (≤), (>), (≥)       ::  a → a → Bool
   min, max                 ::  a → a → a

   min x y | x ≤ y    =  x
           | otherwise  =  y
   max x y | x ≤ y    =  y
           | otherwise  =  x
```

That is, for a type to be an instance of *Ord* it must be an instance of *Eq*, and support six additional operators. Because default definitions have already been included for *min* and *max*, declaring an equality type (such as *Bool*) as an ordered type only requires defining the four comparison operators:

```
instance Ord Bool where
   False < True  =  True
   _ < _         =  False

   b ≤ c         =  (b < c) ∨ (b == c)
   b > c         =  c < b
   b ≥ c         =  c ≤ b
```

Derived instances

When new types are declared, it is usually appropriate to make them into instances of a number of built-in classes. Haskell provides a simple facility for automatically making new types into instances of the classes *Eq*, *Ord*, *Show*, and *Read*, in the form of the **deriving** mechanism. For example, the type *Bool* is actually declared in the standard library as follows:

```
data Bool  =  False | True
                deriving (Eq, Ord, Show, Read)
```

As a result, all the member functions from the four derived classes can then be used with logical values. For example:

```
> False == False
True
```

```
> False < True
True
```

```
> show False
"False"
```

```
> read "False" :: Bool
False
```

The use of :: in the last example is required to resolve the type of the result, which in this case cannot be inferred from the context. Note that for the purposes of deriving instances of the class *Ord* of ordered types, the ordering on the constructors of a type is determined by their position in its declaration.

Hence, the above declaration for the type *Bool*, in which *False* appears before *True*, results in the ordering *False < True*.

In the case of constructors with arguments, the types of these arguments must also be instances of any derived classes. For example, recall the following declarations from earlier in this chapter:

> **data** *Shape*   =   *Circle Float | Rect Float Float*
>
> **data** *Maybe a* = *Nothing | Just a*

To derive *Shape* as an equality type requires that the type *Float* is also an equality type, which is indeed the case. Similarly, to derive *Maybe a* as an equality type requires that the type *a* is also such a type, which then becomes a class constraint on this parameter. In the same manner as lists and tuples, values built using constructors with arguments are ordered lexicographically. For example, if *Shape* is derived as an ordered type, then we have:

> `> Rect 1.0 4.0 < Rect 2.0 3.0`
> *True*

> `> Rect 1.0 4.0 < Rect 1.0 3.0`
> *False*

Monadic types

We conclude this chapter by returning once again to parsers and interactive programs, the subjects of the previous two chapters. As the reader may recall, the functions *return* and $\ggg$ were defined for both parsers,

> *return* :: *a → Parser a*
>
> ($\ggg$)   :: *Parser a → (a → Parser b) → Parser b*

and interactive programs:

> *return* :: *a → IO a*
>
> ($\ggg$) :: *IO a → (a → IO b) → IO b*

The use of the same function names and analagous types is not coincidental. In particular, generalising from the specific cases of *Parser* and *IO* to an arbitrary parameterised type gives the notion of a *monad*, which in Haskell is captured by the following class declaration:

> **class** *Monad m* **where**
>
>   *return* :: *a → m a*
>
>   ($\ggg$)   :: *m a → (a → m b) → m b*

That is, a monad is a parameterised type *m* that supports *return* and $\ggg$ functions of the specified types. The fact that *m* must be a parameterised type, rather than just a type, is inferred from its use in the types for the two functions. Using this declaration, parsers and interactive programs can then be made into instances of the class of monadic types, by defining the two member functions in the appropriate manner:

```
instance Monad Parser where
    return v  =  ···
    p >>= f   =  ···
instance Monad IO where
    return v  =  ···
    f >>= g   =  ···
```

It is because of these declarations that the **do** notation can be used to sequence parsers and interactive programs. More generally, Haskell supports the use of this notation with any monadic type, allowing expressions of the form

$$e1 \gg= \lambda v1 \rightarrow$$
$$e2 \gg= \lambda v2 \rightarrow$$
$$\vdots$$
$$en \gg= \lambda vn \rightarrow$$
$$return\ (f\ v1\ v2\ ...\ vn)$$

to be written as:

do $v1 \leftarrow e1$
   $v2 \leftarrow e2$
   $\vdots$
   $vn \leftarrow en$
   $return\ (f\ v1\ v2\ ...\ vn)$

10.7 | Chapter remarks

The abstract machine example is derived from (19), and the type of control stacks used in this example is a special case of the zipper data structure for traversing values of recursive types (12). The term *monad* comes from a branch of mathematics known as category theory (23). For further details on the theory and application of monads in functional programming, see (31; 24). As well as the basic mechanisms for declaring new types and classes introduced in this chapter, the Hugs system also supports a number of more advanced and experimental typing features; see *www.haskell.org/hugs*.

10.8 | Exercises

1. Using recursion and the function *add*, define a multiplication function $mult :: Nat \rightarrow Nat \rightarrow Nat$ for natural numbers.

2. Although not included in appendix A, the standard library defines

data $Ordering = LT\ |\ EQ\ |\ GT$

together with a function

$compare\ ::\ Ord\ a \Rightarrow a \rightarrow a \rightarrow Ordering$

that decides if one value in an ordered type is less than (LT), equal to (EQ), or greater than (GT) another such value. Using this function, redefine the function $occurs :: Int \rightarrow Tree \rightarrow Bool$ for search trees. Why is this new definition more efficient than the original version?

3. Consider the following type of binary trees:

> **type** $Tree$ = $Leaf\ Int \mid Node\ Tree\ Tree$

Let us say that such a tree is *balanced* if the number of leaves in the left and right subtree of every node differs by at most one, with leaves themselves being trivially balanced. Define a function $balanced :: Tree \rightarrow Bool$ that decides if a tree is balanced or not. Hint: first define a function that returns the number of leaves in a tree.

4. Define a function $balance :: [Int] \rightarrow Tree$ that converts a non-empty list of integers into a balanced tree. Hint: first define a function that splits a list into two halves whose length differs by at most one.

5. Extend the tautology checker to support the use of logical disjunction ($\vee$) and equivalence ($\Leftrightarrow$) in propositions.

6. Using the function $isTaut$ together with the parsing and interaction libraries from the previous two chapters, define an interactive tautology checker that allows propositions to be entered from the keyboard in a user-friendly syntax. Hint: build a parser for propositions by modifying the parser for arithmetic expressions given in chapter 8.

7. Extend the abstract machine to support the use of multiplication.

8. Complete the following instance declarations:

> **instance** $Monad\ Maybe$ **where**
>
> $\quad$ . . .
>
> **instance** $Monad\ []$ **where**
>
> $\quad$ . . .

In this context, [ ] denotes the list type [a] without its parameter. Hint: first write down the types of $return$ and $\ggg=$ for each instance.

chapter 11

The countdown problem

In this chapter we show how Haskell can be used to solve the countdown problem, a numbers game in which the aim is to construct numeric expressions satisfying certain constraints. We start by formalising the rules of the problem in Haskell, and then present a simple but inefficient program that solves the problem, whose efficiency is then improved in two stages.

11.1 | Introduction

Countdown is a popular quiz programme that has been running on British television since 1982, and includes a numbers game that we shall refer to as the *countdown problem*. The essence of the problem is as follows:

> Given a sequence of numbers and a target number, attempt to construct an expression whose value is the target, by combining one or more numbers from the sequence using addition, subtraction, multiplication, division and parentheses.

Each number in the sequence can only be used at most once in the expression, and all of the numbers involved, including intermediate values, must be positive natural numbers $(1, 2, 3, \ldots)$. In particular, the use of negative numbers, zero, and proper fractions such as $2 \div 3$, is not permitted.

For example, suppose that we are given the sequence $1, 3, 7, 10, 25, 50$, and the target 765. Then one possible solution is given by the expression $(1 + 50) * (25 - 10)$, as shown by the following simple calculation:

$$
\begin{aligned}
& (1 + 50) * (25 - 10) \\
= \quad & \{ \text{applying} + \} \\
& 51 * (25 - 10) \\
= \quad & \{ \text{applying} - \} \\
& 51 * 15 \\
= \quad & \{ \text{applying} * \} \\
& 765
\end{aligned}
$$

In fact, for this example it can be shown that there are 780 different solutions. On the other hand, keeping the same sequence but changing the target to 831 gives an example that can be shown to have no solutions.

In the television version of the countdown problem, a number of additional rules are adopted to make the problem suitable for human players on a quiz programme. In particular, there are always six numbers selected from the sequence $1 \ldots 10, 1 \ldots 10, 25, 50, 75, 100$, the target is always in the range $100 \ldots 999$, and there is a time limit of 30 seconds. It is natural to abstract from such constraints when developing a computer player, so none of the programs that we develop in this chapter enforces or depends upon these extra rules. Note, however, that we do not abstract from the positive naturals to a richer numeric domain such as the integers or rationals, as this would fundamentally change the computational complexity of the problem.

11.2 | Formalising the problem

We start by defining a type for the four numeric operators:

$$\textbf{data } Op \quad = \quad Add \mid Sub \mid Mul \mid Div$$

Using this type, we define a function *valid* that decides if the application of an operator to two positive naturals gives another positive natural, and a function *apply* that actually performs such a valid application:

$$
\begin{array}{lll}
valid & :: & Op \to Int \to Int \to Bool \\
valid\ Add\ \_\ \_ & = & True \\
valid\ Sub\ x\ y & = & x > y \\
valid\ Mul\ \_\ \_ & = & True \\
valid\ Div\ x\ y & = & x\ `mod`\ y == 0 \\
\\
apply & :: & Op \to Int \to Int \to Int \\
apply\ Add\ x\ y & = & x + y \\
apply\ Sub\ x\ y & = & x - y \\
apply\ Mul\ x\ y & = & x * y \\
apply\ Div\ x\ y & = & x\ `div`\ y
\end{array}
$$

For example, the application $Sub\ 2\ 3$ is invalid because $2 - 3$ is negative, while $Div\ 2\ 3$ is invalid because $2 \div 3$ is rational. In turn, we define a type for numeric expressions, which can either be an integer value or the application of an operator to two argument expressions:

$$\textbf{data } Expr \quad = \quad Val\ Int \mid App\ Op\ Expr\ Expr$$

Using this type, we define a function that returns the list of *values* in an expression, and a function *eval* that returns the overall value of an expression, provided that this value is a positive natural number:

$$
\begin{array}{lll}
values & :: & Expr \rightarrow [\,Int\,] \\
values\ (Val\ n) & = & [\,n\,] \\
values\ (App\ \_\ l\ r) & = & values\ l \mathbin{+\!\!+} values\ r \\[4pt]
eval & :: & Expr \rightarrow [\,Int\,] \\
eval\ (Val\ n) & = & [\,n \mid n > 0\,] \\
eval\ (App\ o\ l\ r) & = & [\,apply\ o\ x\ y \mid x \leftarrow eval\ l, \\
& & \qquad\qquad\qquad y \leftarrow eval\ r, \\
& & \qquad\qquad\qquad valid\ o\ x\ y\,]
\end{array}
$$

Note that the possibility of failure within $eval$ is handled by returning a list of results, with the convention that a singleton list denotes success, and the empty list denotes failure. For example, for $2 + 3$ and $2 - 3$, we have:

```
>  eval (App Add (Val 2) (Val 3))
[5]
```

```
>  eval (App Sub (Val 2) (Val 3))
[]
```

Failure within $eval$ could also be handled by using the $Maybe$ type, but we prefer to use the list type in this case because the comprehension notation then provides a convenient way to define the $eval$ function.

We now define a number of useful combinatorial functions that return all possible lists satisfying certain properties. The function $subs$ returns all subsequences of a list, which are given by all possible combinations of excluding or including each element, $interleave$ returns all possible ways of inserting a new element into a list, and $perms$ returns all permutations of a list, which are given by all possible reorderings of the elements:

$$
\begin{array}{lll}
subs & :: & [\,a\,] \rightarrow [[\,a\,]] \\
subs\ [\,] & = & [[\,]] \\
subs\ (x : xs) & = & yss \mathbin{+\!\!+} map\ (x:)\ yss \\
& & \mathbf{where}\ yss = subs\ xs \\[4pt]
interleave & :: & a \rightarrow [\,a\,] \rightarrow [[\,a\,]] \\
interleave\ x\ [\,] & = & [[\,x\,]] \\
interleave\ x\ (y : ys) & = & (x : y : ys) : map\ (y:)\ (interleave\ x\ ys) \\[4pt]
perms & :: & [\,a\,] \rightarrow [[\,a\,]] \\
perms\ [\,] & = & [[\,]] \\
perms\ (x : xs) & = & concat\ (map\ (interleave\ x)\ (perms\ xs))
\end{array}
$$

For example:

```
>  subs [1, 2, 3]
[[], [3], [2], [2, 3], [1], [1, 3], [1, 2], [1, 2, 3]]
```

```
>  interleave 1 [2, 3, 4]
[[1, 2, 3, 4], [2, 1, 3, 4], [2, 3, 1, 4], [2, 3, 4, 1]]
```

```
>  perms [1, 2, 3]
[[1, 2, 3], [2, 1, 3], [2, 3, 1], [1, 3, 2], [3, 1, 2], [3, 2, 1]]
```

In turn, a function that returns all *choices* from a list, which are given by all possible ways of selecting zero or more elements in any order, can then be defined simply by considering all permutations of all subsequences:

$$
\begin{aligned}
choices &:: [a] \rightarrow [[a]] \\
choices\ xs &= concat\ (map\ perms\ (subs\ xs))
\end{aligned}
$$

For example:

> $choices\ [1, 2, 3]$
[[ ], [3], [2], [2, 3], [3, 2], [1], [1, 3], [3, 1], [1, 2], [2, 1],
[1, 2, 3], [2, 1, 3], [2, 3, 1], [1, 3, 2], [3, 1, 2], [3, 2, 1]]

Finally, we can now define a function *solution* that formalises what it means to solve an instance of the countdown problem:

$$
\begin{aligned}
solution &:: Expr \rightarrow [Int] \rightarrow Int \rightarrow Bool \\
solution\ e\ ns\ n &= elem\ (values\ e)\ (choices\ ns) \wedge eval\ e == [n]
\end{aligned}
$$

That is, an expression is a solution for a given list of numbers and a target if the list of values in the expression is chosen from the list of numbers, and the expression successfully evaluates to give the target. For example, if $e :: Expr$ represents the expression $(1 + 50) * (25 - 10)$, then we have:

> $solution\ e\ [1, 3, 7, 10, 25, 50]\ 765$
True

The efficiency of *solution* could be improved by using a function *isChoice* that decides directly if one list is chosen from another, rather than doing so indirectly using the function *choices* that returns all possible choices from a list. However, efficiency is not important at this stage, and *choices* itself is used to define a number of other functions in this chapter.

11.3 | Brute force solution

Our first approach to solving the countdown problem is by brute force, using the idea of generating all possible expressions over the given list of numbers. We start by defining a function *split* that returns all possible ways of splitting a list into two non-empty lists that append to give the original list:

$$
\begin{aligned}
split &:: [a] \rightarrow [([a], [a])] \\
split\ [] &= [] \\
split\ [\_] &= [] \\
split\ (x : xs) &= ([x], xs) : [(x : ls, rs) \mid (ls, rs) \leftarrow split\ xs]
\end{aligned}
$$

For example:

> $split\ [1, 2, 3, 4]$
[([1], [2, 3, 4]), ([1, 2], [3, 4]), ([1, 2, 3], [4])]

Using *split* we can then define the key function, *exprs*, which returns all possible expressions whose list of values is precisely a given list:

$$
\begin{aligned}
exprs \quad &:: \quad [Int] \rightarrow [Expr] \\
exprs\ [\,] \quad &= \quad [\,] \\
exprs\ [n] \quad &= \quad [Val\ n] \\
exprs\ ns \quad &= \quad [e \mid (ls, rs) \leftarrow split\ ns, \\
&\qquad\qquad l \leftarrow exprs\ ls, \\
&\qquad\qquad r \leftarrow exprs\ rs, \\
&\qquad\qquad e \leftarrow combine\ l\ r]
\end{aligned}
$$

That is, for the empty list of numbers there are no possible expressions, while for a single number there is a single expression comprising that number. Otherwise, for a list of two or more numbers we first produce all splittings of the list, then recursively calculate all possible expressions for each of these lists, and, finally, combine each pair of expressions using each of the four numeric operators, using an auxiliary function defined as follows:

$$
\begin{aligned}
combine \quad &:: \quad Expr \rightarrow Expr \rightarrow [Expr] \\
combine\ l\ r \quad &= \quad [App\ o\ l\ r \mid o \leftarrow ops] \\
\\
ops \quad &:: \quad [Op] \\
ops \quad &= \quad [Add, Sub, Mul, Div]
\end{aligned}
$$

Finally, we can now define a function *solutions* that returns all possible expressions that solve an instance of the countdown problem, by first generating all expressions over each choice from the given list of numbers, and then selecting those expressions that successfully evaluate to give the target:

$$
\begin{aligned}
solutions \quad &:: \quad [Int] \rightarrow Int \rightarrow [Expr] \\
solutions\ ns\ n \quad &= \quad [e \mid ns' \leftarrow choices\ ns, \\
&\qquad\qquad e \leftarrow exprs\ ns', \\
&\qquad\qquad eval\ e == [n]]
\end{aligned}
$$

For the purposes of testing our programs in this chapter, the performance of Hugs is somewhat limited, so instead we use the Glasgow Haskell Compiler. For example, using GHC version 6.4.1 on a 1.2GHz Pentium M laptop, *solutions* $[1, 3, 7, 10, 25, 50]$ 765 returns the first solution in 0.36 seconds, and all 780 solutions in 43.98 seconds, while if the target is changed to 831, then the empty list of solutions is returned in 44.42 seconds.

11.4 | Combining generation and evaluation

The function *solutions* generates all possible expressions over the given numbers, but in practice many of these expressions will fail to evaluate, due to the fact that subtraction and division are not always valid for positive naturals. For example, it can be shown that there are $33,665,406$ possible expressions over the numbers 1, 3, 7, 10, 25, 50, but only $4,672,540$ of these expressions evaluate successfully, which is just under 14%.

Based upon this observation, our second approach to solving the countdown problem is to improve our brute force program by combining the generation of expressions with their evaluation, such that both tasks are performed simultaneously. In this way, expressions that fail to evaluate are rejected at an earlier stage, and, more importantly, are not used to generate further such expressions.

We start by declaring a type *Result* of expressions that evaluate successfully paired with their overall values:

type *Result* = (*Expr*, *Int*)

Using this type, we then define a function *results* that returns all possible results comprising expressions whose list of values is precisely a given list:

$$
\begin{aligned}
&results &&:: \quad [\,Int\,] \rightarrow [\,Result\,] \\
&results\ [\,] &&= \quad [\,] \\
&results\ [n\,] &&= \quad [(\,Val\ n,\,n) \mid n > 0] \\
&results\ ns &&= \quad [\,res \mid (ls,\,rs) \leftarrow split\ ns, \\
&&&\qquad\qquad lx \leftarrow results\ ls, \\
&&&\qquad\qquad ry \leftarrow results\ rs, \\
&&&\qquad\qquad res \leftarrow combine'\ lx\ ry\,]
\end{aligned}
$$

That is, for the empty list there are no possible results, while for a single number there is a single result formed from that number, provided that the number itself is a positive natural. Otherwise, for two or more numbers we first produce all splittings of the list, then recursively calculate all possible results for each of these lists, and, finally, combine each pair of results using each of the four numeric operators that are valid:

$$
\begin{aligned}
&combine' &&:: \quad Result \rightarrow Result \rightarrow [\,Result\,] \\
&combine'\ (l,\,x)\ (r,\,y) &&= \quad [(App\ o\ l\ r,\,apply\ o\ x\ y) \mid o \leftarrow ops, \\
&&&\qquad\qquad\qquad\qquad\quad valid\ o\ x\ y\,]
\end{aligned}
$$

Using *results* we can now define a new function *solutions'* that returns all possible expressions that solve an instance of the countdown problem, by first generating all results over each choice from the given numbers, and then selecting those expressions whose value is the target:

$$
\begin{aligned}
&solutions' &&:: \quad [\,Int\,] \rightarrow Int \rightarrow [\,Expr\,] \\
&solutions'\ ns\ n &&= \quad [\,e \mid ns' \leftarrow choices\ ns, \\
&&&\qquad\qquad (e,\,m) \leftarrow results\ ns', \\
&&&\qquad\qquad m == n\,]
\end{aligned}
$$

In terms of performance, *solutions'* $[1, 3, 7, 10, 25, 50]$ 765 returns the first solution in 0.04 seconds (9 times faster than *solutions*) and all solutions in 3.47 seconds (12 times faster), while if the target is changed to 831, the empty list is returned in 3.28 seconds (13 times faster).

11.5 | Exploiting algebraic properties

The function *solutions'* generates all possible expressions over the given numbers whose evaluation is successful, but in practice many of these expressions will be essentially the same, due to the fact that the numeric operators have algebraic properties. For example, the expressions $2 + 3$ and $3 + 2$ are essentially the same because the result of an addition does not depend upon the order of the two arguments, while $2 \div 1$ and 2 are essentially the same because dividing any number by one has no effect on that number.

Based upon this observation, our final approach to solving the countdown problem is to improve our second program by exploiting such properties to reduce the number of generated expressions. In particular, we exploit the following five commutativity and identity properties:

$$
\begin{aligned}
x + y &= y + x \\
x * y &= y * x \\
x * 1 &= x \\
1 * y &= y \\
x \div 1 &= x
\end{aligned}
$$

We start by recalling the function *valid* that decides if the application of an operator to two positive naturals gives another such:

$$
\begin{aligned}
valid \quad &:: \quad Op \rightarrow Int \rightarrow Int \rightarrow Bool \\
valid\ Add\ \_\ \_ &= \quad True \\
valid\ Sub\ x\ y &= \quad x > y \\
valid\ Mul\ \_\ \_ &= \quad True \\
valid\ Div\ x\ y &= \quad x\ `mod`\ y == 0
\end{aligned}
$$

This definition can be modified to exploit the commutativity of addition and multiplication simply by requiring that their arguments are in numeric order ($x \leq y$), and the identity properties of multiplication and division simply by requiring that the appropriate arguments are non-unitary ($\neq 1$):

$$
\begin{aligned}
valid\ Add\ x\ y &= \quad x \leq y \\
valid\ Sub\ x\ y &= \quad x > y \\
valid\ Mul\ x\ y &= \quad x \neq 1 \wedge y \neq 1 \wedge x \leq y \\
valid\ Div\ x\ y &= \quad y \neq 1 \wedge x\ `mod`\ y == 0
\end{aligned}
$$

For example, using this new definition, *Add* 3 2 is now invalid because it is essentially the same as *Add* 2 3 using the commutativity of addition, while *Div* 2 1 is now invalid because it is essentially the same as the number 2 on its own using the identity property for division.

Using the new version of *valid* gives a new version of our function *solutions'* that solves the countdown problem, which we write as *solutions''*. Using this new function can considerably reduce the number of generated expressions and the number of solutions. For example, *solutions''* [1, 3, 7, 10, 25, 50] 765 only generates 245, 644 expressions, of which just 49 are solutions, which is just over 5% and 6% respectively of the numbers using *solutions'*.

As regards performance, *solutions''* [1, 3, 7, 10, 25, 50] 765 now returns the first solution in 0.02 seconds (twice as fast as *solutions'*) and all solutions in 0.44 seconds (7 times faster), while for the target number 831 the empty list is also returned in 0.44 seconds (7 times faster). More generally, given any numbers from the television version of the countdown problem, our final program *solutions''* typically returns all solutions in under one second.

11.6 | Chapter remarks

Countdown is based upon an original version on French television called "Des Chiffres et des Lettres", while the countdown problem itself is related to the childrens arithmetic games called "krypto" and "four fours". This chapter is based upon (15), which also includes proofs of correctness of the three programs produced. A number of more advanced approaches to solving the countdown problem are explored by Bird and Mu (2). The definitions for the functions *subs*, *interleave*, and *perms* are due to Bird and Wadler (3).

11.7 | Exercises

1. Redefine the combinatorial function *choices* using a list comprehension rather than the library functions *concat* and *map*.

2. Define a recursive function $isChoice :: Eq\ a \Rightarrow [a] \rightarrow [a] \rightarrow Bool$ that decides if one list is chosen from another, without using the combinatorial functions *perms* and *subs*. Hint: start by defining a function that removes the first occurrence of a value from a list.

3. What effect would generalising the function *split* to also return pairs containing the empty list have on the behaviour of *solutions*?

4. Using *choices*, *exprs*, and *eval*, verify that there are $33,665,406$ possible expressions over the numbers $1, 3, 7, 10, 25, 50$, and that only $4,672,540$ of these expressions evaluate successfully.

5. Similarly, verify that the number of expressions that evaluate successfully increases to $10,839,369$ if the numeric domain is generalised to arbitrary integers. Hint: modify the definition of *valid*.

6. Modify the final program to:

   (a) allow the use of exponentiation in expressions;
   (b) produce the nearest solutions if no exact solution is possible;
   (c) order the solutions using a suitable measure of simplicity.

chapter 12

Lazy evaluation

In this chapter we introduce lazy evaluation, the mechanism used to evaluate expressions in Haskell. We start by reviewing the notion of evaluation, then consider evaluation strategies and their properties, discuss infinite structures and modular programming, and conclude with a special form of function application that can improve the space performance of programs.

12.1 | Introduction

As we have seen throughout this book, the basic method of computation in Haskell is the application of functions to arguments. For example, suppose that we define a function that increments an integer:

$$
\begin{aligned}
inc &:: & Int \to Int \\
inc\ n &= & n + 1
\end{aligned}
$$

Then the expression $inc\ (2 * 3)$ can be evaluated as follows:

$$
\begin{aligned}
& inc\ (2 * 3) \\
= &\quad \{\ \text{applying } *\ \} \\
& inc\ 6 \\
= &\quad \{\ \text{applying } inc\ \} \\
& 6 + 1 \\
= &\quad \{\ \text{applying } +\ \} \\
& 7
\end{aligned}
$$

Alternatively, the same result can also be obtained by performing the first two function applications in the opposite order:

$$
\begin{aligned}
& inc\ (2 * 3) \\
= &\quad \{\ \text{applying } inc\ \} \\
& (2 * 3) + 1 \\
= &\quad \{\ \text{applying } *\ \} \\
& 6 + 1 \\
= &\quad \{\ \text{applying } +\ \}
\end{aligned}
$$

7

The fact that changing the order in which functions are applied does not affect the final result is not specific to such simple examples, but is an important general property of function application in Haskell. More formally, in Haskell any two different ways of evaluating the same expression will always produce the same final value, provided that they both terminate. We will return to the issue of termination later on in this chapter.

Note that the above property does not hold for most imperative programming languages, in which the basic method of computation is changing stored values. For example, consider the imperative expression $n + (n := 1)$ that adds the current value of the variable n to the result of changing its value to one, assuming that n initially has the value zero. This expression can be evaluated by first performing the left-hand side of the addition

$$
\begin{aligned}
& n + (n := 1) \\
=\ & \{ \text{applying } n \} \\
& 0 + (n := 1) \\
=\ & \{ \text{applying} := \} \\
& 0 + 1 \\
=\ & \{ \text{applying} + \} \\
& 1
\end{aligned}
$$

or alternatively, by first performing the right-hand side:

$$
\begin{aligned}
& n + (n := 1) \\
=\ & \{ \text{applying} := \} \\
& n + 1 \\
=\ & \{ \text{applying } n \} \\
& 1 + 1 \\
=\ & \{ \text{applying} + \} \\
& 2
\end{aligned}
$$

The final value is different in each case. The general problem illustrated by this example is that the precise time at which an assignment is performed in an imperative language may affect the value that results from a computation. In contrast, the time at which a function is applied to an argument in Haskell never affects the value that results from a computation. Nonetheless, as we shall see in the remainder of this chapter, there are important practical issues concerning the order and nature of evaluation.

12.2 | Evaluation strategies

An expression that has the form of a function applied to one or more arguments that can be "reduced" by performing the application is called a reducible expression, or *redex* for short. As indicated by the use of quotations marks in the preceding sentence, such reductions do not necessarily decrease the size of an expression, although in practice this is often the case.

By way of example, suppose that we define a function *mult* that takes a pair of integers and returns their product:

$$mult \quad\quad :: \quad (Int, Int) \rightarrow Int$$
$$mult \, (x, y) \quad = \quad x * y$$

Now consider the expression $mult \, (1 + 2, 2 + 3)$. This expression contains three redexes, namely the sub-expressions $1 + 2$ and $2 + 3$, which have the form of the function $+$ applied to two arguments, and the entire expression $mult \, (1 + 2, 2 + 3)$ itself, which has the form of the function $mult$ applied to a pair of arguments. Performing the corresponding reductions gives the expressions $mult \, (3, 2 + 3)$, $mult \, (1 + 2, 5)$, and $(1 + 2) * (2 + 3)$.

When evaluating an expression, in what order should reductions be performed? One common strategy, called *innermost* evaluation, is to always choose a redex that is innermost, in the sense that it contains no other redex. If there is more than one innermost redex, by convention we choose that which begins at the leftmost position in the expression.

For example, both $1 + 2$ and $2 + 3$ contain no other redexes and are hence innermost within the expression $mult \, (1 + 2, 2 + 3)$, with the redex $1 + 2$ beginning at the leftmost position. More generally, our example expression is evaluated using innermost evaluation as follows:

$$mult \, (1 + 2, 2 + 3)$$
$$= \quad \{ \text{applying the first } + \}$$
$$mult \, (3, 2 + 3)$$
$$= \quad \{ \text{applying } + \}$$
$$mult \, (3, 5)$$
$$= \quad \{ \text{applying } mult \}$$
$$3 * 5$$
$$= \quad \{ \text{applying } * \}$$
$$15$$

Innermost evaluation can also be characterised in terms of how arguments are passed to functions. In particular, using this strategy ensures that the argument of a function is always fully evaluated before the function itself is applied. That is, arguments are passed *by value*. For example, as shown above, evaluating $mult \, (1 + 2, 2 + 3)$ using innermost evaluation proceeds by first evaluating the argument expressions $1 + 2$ and $2 + 3$, and then applying the function $mult$. The fact that we always choose the leftmost innermost redex ensures that the first argument is evaluated before the second.

Another common strategy for evaluating an expression, dual to innermost evaluation, is to always choose a redex that is outermost, in the sense that it is contained in no other redex. If there is more than one such redex then as previously we choose that which begins at the leftmost position. Not surprisingly, this evaluation strategy is called *outermost* evaluation.

For example, the expression $mult \, (1 + 2, 2 + 3)$ is contained in no other redex and is hence outermost within itself. More generally, evaluating this expression using outermost evaluation proceeds as follows:

$$mult \, (1 + 2, 2 + 3)$$
$$= \quad \{ \text{applying } mult \}$$
$$(1 + 2) * (2 + 3)$$
$$= \quad \{ \text{applying the first } + \}$$

$$3 * (2 + 3)$$
$$= \quad \{ \text{applying} + \}$$
$$3 * 5$$
$$= \quad \{ \text{applying} * \}$$
$$15$$

In terms of how arguments are passed to functions, using outermost evaluation allows functions to be applied before their arguments are evaluated. For this reason, we say that arguments are passed *by name*. For example, as shown above, evaluating $mult\ (1 + 2, 2 + 3)$ using outermost evaluation proceeds by first applying the function $mult$ to the two unevaluated arguments $1 + 2$ and $2 + 3$, and then evaluating these two expressions in turn.

Note, however, that many built-in functions require their arguments to be evaluated before being applied, even when using outermost evaluation. For example, as illustrated in the calculation above, built-in arithmetic operators such as $*$ and $+$ cannot be applied until their two arguments have been evaluated to numbers. Functions with this property are called strict, and will be discussed in further detail at the end of this chapter.

Lambda expressions

Let us now define a curried version of $mult$ that takes its arguments one at a time, using a lambda expression to make the use of currying explicit:

$$mult \quad :: \quad Int \to Int \to Int$$
$$mult\ x \ = \ \lambda y \to x * y$$

Then using innermost evaluation, for example, we have:

$$mult\ (1 + 2)\ (2 + 3)$$
$$= \quad \{ \text{applying the first} + \}$$
$$mult\ 3\ (2 + 3)$$
$$= \quad \{ \text{applying } mult \}$$
$$(\lambda y \to 3 * y)\ (2 + 3)$$
$$= \quad \{ \text{applying} + \}$$
$$(\lambda y \to 3 * y)\ 5$$
$$= \quad \{ \text{applying } \lambda y \to 3 * y \}$$
$$3 * 5$$
$$= \quad \{ \text{applying} * \}$$
$$15$$

That is, the two arguments are now substituted into the body of the function $mult$ one at a time, as we would expect using currying, rather than at the same time as in the previous section. This behaviour arises because $mult\ 3$ is the leftmost innermost redex in the expression $mult\ 3\ (2 + 3)$, as opposed to $2 + 3$ in the expression $mult\ (3, 2 + 3)$. Performing a reduction on $mult\ 3$ in the second step of the calculation above gives the lambda expression $(\lambda y \to 3 * y)$, which awaits the result of evaluating the second argument.

Note that in Haskell, the selection of redexes within lambda expressions is prohibited. The rational for not "reducing under lambdas" is that functions are viewed as black boxes that we are not permitted to look inside. More formally, the only operation that can be performed on a function is that of applying it to an argument. As such, reduction within the body of a function is only permitted once the function has been applied. For example, the lambda expression $\lambda x \to 1 + 2$ is deemed to be fully evaluated, even though its body contains the redex $1 + 2$, but once this function has been applied to an argument, evaluation of this redex can then proceed:

$$
\begin{aligned}
& (\lambda x \to 1 + 2)\, 0 \\
= \quad & \{ \text{applying } \lambda x \to 1 + 2 \} \\
& 1 + 2 \\
= \quad & \{ \text{applying } + \} \\
& 3
\end{aligned}
$$

Using innermost and outermost evaluation, but not under lambdas, is normally referred to as *call-by-value* and *call-by-name* evaluation, respectively. In the next two sections we explore how these two evaluation strategies compare in terms of two important properties, namely their termination behaviour and the number of reduction steps that they require.

12.3 | Termination

Consider the following recursive definition:

$$
\begin{aligned}
inf \quad &:: \quad Int \\
inf \quad &= \quad 1 + inf
\end{aligned}
$$

That is, the integer *inf* (abbreviating "infinity") is defined as the successor of itself. Evaluating *inf* produces a larger and larger expression, regardless of the evaluation strategy, and hence does not terminate:

$$
\begin{aligned}
& inf \\
= \quad & \{ \text{applying } inf \} \\
& 1 + inf \\
= \quad & \{ \text{applying } inf \} \\
& 1 + (1 + inf) \\
= \quad & \{ \text{applying } inf \} \\
& 1 + (1 + (1 + inf)) \\
= \quad & \{ \text{applying } inf \} \\
& \vdots
\end{aligned}
$$

In practice, evaluating *inf* using Hugs will quickly exhaust the available memory and produce an error message. Now consider the expression *fst* $(0, inf)$, where *fst* is the library function that selects the first component of a pair, defined by *fst* $(x, y) = x$. Using call-by-value evaluation with this expression also results in non-termination in a similar manner:

$$
\begin{aligned}
& fst\, (0, inf) \\
= \quad & \{ \text{applying } inf \} \\
& fst\, (0, 1 + inf)
\end{aligned}
$$

$$= \quad \{ \text{applying } \mathit{inf} \}$$
$$\mathit{fst} \ (0, 1 + (1 + \mathit{inf}))$$
$$= \quad \{ \text{applying } \mathit{inf} \}$$
$$\mathit{fst} \ (0, 1 + (1 + (1 + \mathit{inf})))$$
$$= \quad \{ \text{applying } \mathit{inf} \}$$
$$\vdots$$

In contrast, using call-by-name evaluation results in termination in just one step, by immediately applying the definition of *fst* and hence avoiding the evaluation of the non-terminating expression *inf*:

$$\mathit{fst} \ (0, \ \mathit{inf})$$
$$= \quad \{ \text{applying } \mathit{fst} \}$$
$$0$$

This simple example shows that call-by-name evaluation may produce a result when call-by-value evaluation fails to terminate. More generally, we have the following important property: if there exists any evaluation sequence that terminates for a given expression, then call-by-name evaluation will also terminate for this expression, and produce the same final result.

In summary, call-by-name evaluation is preferable to call-by-value for the purpose of ensuring that evaluation terminates as often as possible.

12.4 | Number of reductions

Now consider the following definition:

$$\begin{aligned} \mathit{square} \quad &:: \quad \mathit{Int} \rightarrow \mathit{Int} \\ \mathit{square} \ n \ &= \quad n * n \end{aligned}$$

For example, using call-by-value evaluation, we have:

$$\mathit{square} \ (1 + 2)$$
$$= \quad \{ \text{applying} + \}$$
$$\mathit{square} \ 3$$
$$= \quad \{ \text{applying } \mathit{square} \}$$
$$3 * 3$$
$$= \quad \{ \text{applying} * \}$$
$$9$$

In contrast, using call-by-name evaluation with the same expression requires one extra reduction step, due to the fact that $1 + 2$ is duplicated when the function *square* is applied, and hence must be evaluated twice:

$$\mathit{square} \ (1 + 2)$$
$$= \quad \{ \text{applying } \mathit{square} \}$$
$$(1 + 2) * (1 + 2)$$
$$= \quad \{ \text{applying the first} + \}$$
$$3 * (1 + 2)$$
$$= \quad \{ \text{applying} + \}$$

$$3 * 3$$
$$= \quad \{ \text{applying } * \}$$
$$9$$

This example shows that call-by-name evaluation may require more steps than call-by-value evaluation, in particular when an argument is used more than once in the body of a function. More generally, we have the following property: arguments are evaluated precisely once using call-by-value evaluation, but may be evaluated many times using call-by-name.

Fortunately, the above efficiency problem with call-by-name evaluation can easily be solved, by using pointers to indicate sharing of expressions during evaluation. Rather than physically copying an argument if it is used many times in the body of a function, we simply keep one copy of the argument and make many pointers to it. In this manner, any reductions that are performed on the argument are automatically shared between each of the pointers to that argument. For example, using this strategy we have:

$$square \ (1 + 2)$$

$$= \quad \{ \text{applying } square \}$$

$$= \quad \{ \text{applying } + \}$$

$$= \quad \{ \text{applying } * \}$$

$$9$$

That is, when applying the definition $square \ n = n * n$ in the first step, we keep a single copy of the argument expression $1 + 2$, and make two pointers to it. In this manner, when the expression $1 + 2$ is reduced in the second step, both pointers in the expression share the result.

The use of call-by-name evaluation in conjunction with sharing is called *lazy evaluation*. This is the evaluation strategy that is used in Haskell, as a result of which Haskell is called a lazy programming language. Being based upon call-by-name evaluation, lazy evaluation has the property that it ensures that evaluation terminates as often as possible. Moreover, using sharing ensures that lazy evaluation never requires more steps than call-by-value evaluation. The use of the term "lazy" will be explained shortly.

12.5 | Infinite structures

An additional property of call-by-name evaluation, and hence lazy evaluation, is that it allows what at first sight may seem impossible: programming with infinite structures. We have already seen a simple example of this idea earlier in this chapter, in the form of the evaluation of $fst \ (0, inf)$ avoiding the production of the infinite structure $1 + (1 + (1 + \cdots))$ defined by inf.

More interesting forms of behaviour occur when we consider infinite lists. For example, consider the following recursive definition:

$$ones \quad :: \quad [Int]$$
$$ones \quad = \quad 1 : ones$$

That is, the list *ones* is defined as a single one followed by itself. As with *inf*, evaluating *ones* does not terminate, regardless of the strategy used:

$$
\begin{array}{ll}
& ones \\
= & \{ \text{applying } ones \} \\
& 1 : ones \\
= & \{ \text{applying } ones \} \\
& 1 : (1 : ones) \\
= & \{ \text{applying } ones \} \\
& 1 : (1 : (1 : ones)) \\
= & \{ \text{applying } ones \} \\
& \vdots
\end{array}
$$

In practice, evaluating *ones* using Hugs will produce a never-ending list of ones, until the user eventually decides to terminate this process:

$$> \; ones$$
$$[1, 1, 1, 1, 1, 1, 1, 1, 1, 1, 1, \cdots$$

Now consider the expression *head ones*, which attempts to select the first element of this infinite list of ones. Using call-by-value evaluation with this expression also results in non-termination:

$$
\begin{array}{ll}
& head \; ones \\
= & \{ \text{applying } ones \} \\
& head \; (1 : ones) \\
= & \{ \text{applying } ones \} \\
& head \; (1 : (1 : ones)) \\
= & \{ \text{applying } ones \} \\
& head \; (1 : (1 : (1 : ones))) \\
= & \{ \text{applying } ones \} \\
& \vdots
\end{array}
$$

In contrast, using lazy evaluation (or call-by-name evaluation, as sharing is not required in this example) results in termination in two steps:

$$
\begin{array}{ll}
& head \; ones \\
= & \{ \text{applying } ones \} \\
& head \; (1 : ones) \\
= & \{ \text{applying } head \} \\
& 1
\end{array}
$$

This behaviour arises because lazy evaluation proceeds in a lazy manner as its name suggests, only evaluating arguments as and when strictly necessary to produce results. For example, when selecting the first element of a list, the remainder of the list is not required, and hence in *head* (1 : *ones*) the further evaluation of the infinite list *ones* is avoided. More generally, we have the following property: using lazy evaluation, expressions are only evaluated as much as required by the context in which they are used.

Using this idea, we now see that under lazy evaluation *ones* is not an infinite list as such, but rather a potentially infinite list, which is only evaluated as much as required by the context. This idea is not restricted to lists, but applies equally to any form of data structure in Haskell. For example, the last exercise for this chapter involves potentially infinite trees.

12.6 | Modular programming

Lazy evaluation also allows us to separate control from data in our computations. For example, a list of three ones can be produced by selecting the first three elements (control) of the infinite list of ones (data):

```
>  take 3 ones
[1, 1, 1]
```

Using the definition of *take* from the standard prelude

$$
\begin{aligned}
take\ 0\ \_ &=\ [\,] \\
take\ (n+1)\ [\,] &=\ [\,] \\
take\ (n+1)\ (x:xs) &=\ x:take\ n\ xs
\end{aligned}
$$

this behaviour arises using lazy evaluation as follows:

$$
\begin{aligned}
&take\ 3\ ones \\
=\quad & \{\ \text{applying}\ ones\ \} \\
&take\ 3\ (1:ones) \\
=\quad & \{\ \text{applying}\ take\ \} \\
&1:take\ 2\ ones \\
=\quad & \{\ \text{applying}\ ones\ \} \\
&1:take\ 2\ (1:ones) \\
=\quad & \{\ \text{applying}\ take\ \} \\
&1:1:take\ 1\ ones \\
=\quad & \{\ \text{applying}\ ones\ \} \\
&1:1:take\ 1\ (1:ones) \\
=\quad & \{\ \text{applying}\ take\ \} \\
&1:1:1:take\ 0\ ones \\
=\quad & \{\ \text{applying}\ take\ \} \\
&1:1:1:[\,] \\
=\quad & \{\ \text{list notation}\ \} \\
&[1, 1, 1]
\end{aligned}
$$

That is, the data is only evaluated as much as required by the control, and these two parts take it in turn to perform reductions. Without lazy evaluation, the control and data parts would need to be combined in the form of a single function that produces a list of n identical elements, such as:

$$
\begin{aligned}
replicate \quad &:: \quad Int \to a \to [\,a\,] \\
replicate\ 0\ \_ \quad &= \quad [\,] \\
replicate\ (n+1)\ x \quad &= \quad x : replicate\ n\ x
\end{aligned}
$$

Being able to modularise programs by separating them into logically distinct parts is an important goal in programming, and being able to separate control from data is one of the most important benefits of lazy evaluation.

Note that care is still required when programming with infinite lists, to avoid non-termination. For example, the expression

$$filter\ (\leq 5)\ [\,1\,..\,]$$

(where $[\,n\,..\,]$ produces the infinite list of integers beginning with n) will produce the integers $1, 2, 3, 4, 5$ and then loop forever, because the function $filter\ (\leq 5)$ keeps testing elements of the infinite list in a vain attempt to find another that is less than or equal to five. In contrast, the expression

$$takeWhile\ (\leq 5)\ [\,1\,..\,]$$

will produce the same integers and then terminate, because $takeWhile\ (\leq 5)$ stops as soon as it finds an element of the list that is greater than five.

We conclude this section with an example concerning prime numbers. In chapter 5 we wrote a function to generate prime numbers up to a given limit. Here is a simple procedure for generating the infinite sequence of all prime numbers, as opposed to some finite prefix of this sequence:

• write down the infinite sequence $2, 3, 4, 5, 6, \cdots$;

• mark the first number, p, in the sequence as prime;

• delete all multiples of p from the sequence;

• return to the second step.

Note that the first and third steps require an infinite amount of work, and hence in practice the steps must be interleaved. The first few iterations of this procedure can be illustrated as follows:

2	3	<u>4</u>	5	<u>6</u>	7	<u>8</u>	9	<u>10</u>	11	<u>12</u>	13	<u>14</u>	15	$\cdots$
	3		5	_	7		<u>9</u>		11	_	13		<u>15</u>	$\cdots$
			5		7			_	11		13		_	$\cdots$
					7				11		13	_		$\cdots$
									11		13			$\cdots$
											13			$\cdots$

Each row corresponds to one iteration, with the first row being the initial sequence (step one), the first number in each row being written in bold to indicate its primality (step two), and all multiples of this number being underlined to indicate their deletion (step three) prior to the next iteration. In this manner, we can imagine the initial sequence of numbers falling downwards, with certain numbers being sieved out at each stage by the underlining, and the bold numbers forming the infinite sequence of primes:

$$2, 3, 5, 7, 11, 13, \cdots$$

The above procedure for generating prime numbers is known as the *sieve of Eratosthenes*, after the Greek mathematician who first described it. This procedure can be translated directly into Haskell:

$$
\begin{array}{lll}
primes & :: & [\mathit{Int}] \\
primes & = & sieve\ [2..] \\[4pt]
sieve & :: & [\mathit{Int}] \rightarrow [\mathit{Int}] \\
sieve\ (p : xs) & = & p : sieve\ [x \mid x \leftarrow xs, x\ `mod`\ p \neq 0]
\end{array}
$$

That is, starting with the infinite list $[2..]$ (step one), we apply the function *sieve* that retains the first number p as being prime (step two), and then calls itself recursively with a new list obtained by filtering all multiples of p from this list (steps three and four). Lazy evaluation ensures that this program does indeed produce the infinite list of all prime numbers:

> *primes*
$[2, 3, 5, 7, 11, 13, 17, 19, 23, 29, 31, 37, 41, 43, 47, 53, 59, 61, 67, \cdots$

By freeing the generation of prime numbers from the constraint of finiteness, we have obtained a modular program on which different control parts can be used in different situations. For example, the first ten prime numbers, and the prime numbers less than ten, can be produced as follows:

> *take* 10 *primes*
$[2, 3, 5, 7, 11, 13, 17, 19, 23, 29]$

> *takeWhile* (<10) *primes*
$[2, 3, 5, 7]$

12.7 | Strict application

Haskell uses lazy evaluation by default, but also provides a special *strict* version of function application, written as $\$!$, which can sometimes be useful. Informally, an expression of the form $f\ \$!\ x$ behaves in the same way as the normal application $f\ x$, except that the top-level of evaluation of the argument expression x is forced before the function f is applied.

For example, if the argument has a basic type, such as *Int* or *Bool*, then top-level evaluation is simply complete evaluation. On the other hand, for a pair type such as $(\mathit{Int}, \mathit{Bool})$, evaluation is performed until a pair of expressions is obtained, but no further. Similarly, for a list type, evaluation is performed until the empty list or the cons of two expressions is obtained.

More formally, an expression of the form $f\ \$!\ x$ is only a redex once evaluation of the argument x, using lazy evaluation as normal, has reached the point where it is known that the result is not an undefined value, at which point the expression can be reduced to the normal application $f\ x$. For example, using the definition $square\ n = n * n$, evaluation of $square\ \$!\ (1 + 2)$ proceeds in a

call-by-value manner, by first evaluating the argument expression $1 + 2$ to give
the value 3, and then applying the function $square$:

$$square \ \$! \ (1 + 2)$$
$$= \quad \{ \text{applying} + \}$$
$$square \ \$! \ 3$$
$$= \quad \{ \text{applying} \ \$! \ \}$$
$$square \ 3$$
$$= \quad \{ \text{applying} \ square \ \}$$
$$3 * 3$$
$$= \quad \{ \text{applying} * \}$$
$$9$$

When used with a curried function with multiple arguments, strict application can be used to force top-level evaluation of any combination of arguments. For example, if f is a curried function with two arguments, an application of the form $f \ x \ y$ can be modified to have three different behaviours:

$$(f \ \$! \ x) \ y \qquad \text{forces top-level evaluation of } x$$
$$(f \ x) \ \$! \ y \qquad \text{forces top-level evaluation of } y$$
$$(f \ \$! \ x) \ \$! \ y \quad \text{forces top-level evaluation of } x \text{ and } y$$

In Haskell, strict application is mainly used to improve the space performance of programs. For example, consider a function $sumwith$ that calculates the sum of a list of integers using an accumulator value:

$$sumwith \qquad\qquad :: \quad Int \to [Int] \to Int$$
$$sumwith \ v \ [] \qquad = \quad v$$
$$sumwith \ v \ (x : xs) \quad = \quad sumwith \ (v + x) \ xs$$

Then using lazy evaluation, we have:

$$sumwith \ 0 \ [1, 2, 3]$$
$$= \quad \{ \text{applying} \ sumwith \ \}$$
$$sumwith \ (0 + 1) \ [2, 3]$$
$$= \quad \{ \text{applying} \ sumwith \ \}$$
$$sumwith \ ((0 + 1) + 2) \ [3]$$
$$= \quad \{ \text{applying} \ sumwith \ \}$$
$$sumwith \ (((0 + 1) + 2) + 3) \ []$$
$$= \quad \{ \text{applying} \ sumwith \ \}$$
$$((0 + 1) + 2) + 3$$
$$= \quad \{ \text{applying the first} + \}$$
$$(1 + 2) + 3$$
$$= \quad \{ \text{applying the first} + \}$$
$$3 + 3$$
$$= \quad \{ \text{applying} + \}$$
$$6$$

Note that the entire summation $((0 + 1) + 2) + 3$ is constructed before any additions are actually performed. More generally, $sumwith$ will construct a summation whose size is proportional to the number of integers in the original list. For example, evaluating $sumwith \ 0 \ [1 .. 10000]$ using Hugs will quickly exhaust the available memory and produce an error message. In practice, it would be preferable to perform each addition as soon as it is introduced, in order to avoid running out of memory in this way.

This behaviour can be achieved by redefining *sumwith* using strict application, to force evaluation of its accumulator value:

$$sumwith\ v\ [\ ] \quad\ =\quad v$$
$$sumwith\ v\ (x:xs)\ =\quad (sumwith\ \$!\ (v+x))\ xs$$

For example, we now have:

$$
\begin{array}{ll}
& sumwith\ 0\ [1,2,3]\\
= & \{\ \text{applying } sumwith\ \}\\
& sumwith\ \$!\ (0+1)\ [2,3]\\
= & \{\ \text{applying } +\ \}\\
& sumwith\ \$!\ 1\ [2,3]\\
= & \{\ \text{applying } \$!\ \}\\
& sumwith\ 1\ [2,3]\\
= & \{\ \text{applying } sumwith\ \}\\
& sumwith\ \$!\ (1+2)\ [3]\\
= & \{\ \text{applying } +\ \}\\
& sumwith\ \$!\ 3\ [3]\\
= & \{\ \text{applying } \$!\ \}\\
& sumwith\ 3\ [3]\\
= & \{\ \text{applying } sumwith\ \}\\
& sumwith\ \$!\ (3+3)\ [\ ]\\
= & \{\ \text{applying } +\ \}\\
& sumwith\ \$!\ 6\ [\ ]\\
= & \{\ \text{applying } \$!\ \}\\
& sumwith\ 6\ [\ ]\\
= & \{\ \text{applying } sumwith\ \}\\
& 6
\end{array}
$$

This evaluation requires more steps than previously, due to the additional overhead of using strict application, but now performs each addition as soon as it is introduced, rather than constructing a large summation. For example, evaluating *sumwith* $0\ [1 .. 10000]$ using Hugs now gives the correct result, as opposed to producing an error as previously.

Generalising from the above example, one may wish to define a strict version of the higher-order library function *foldl* that forces evaluation of its accumulator prior to processing the tail of the list:

$$
\begin{array}{ll}
foldl' & ::\quad (a \to b \to a) \to a \to [b] \to a\\
foldl'\ f\ v\ [\ ] & =\quad v\\
foldl'\ f\ v\ (x:xs) & =\quad ((foldl'\ f)\ \$!\ (f\ v\ x))\ xs
\end{array}
$$

For example, we can now define *sumwith* $= foldl'$ (+). It is important to note, however, that strict application is not a silver bullet that automatically improves the space behaviour of Haskell programs. Even for relatively simple examples, the use of strict application is a specialist topic that requires careful consideration of the behaviour of lazy evaluation.

12.8 | Chapter remarks

Further details about evaluation orders and their properties can be found in (28), and further examples of the use of lazy evaluation for modular programming in the classic *Why Functional Programming Matters* (13). A formal meaning for lazy evaluation is given in (21), and a comprehensive tutorial on the efficient implementation of lazy evaluation in (26).

12.9 | Exercises

1. Identify the redexes in the following expressions, and determine whether each redex is innermost, outermost, neither, or both:

   $1 + (2 * 3)$

   $(1 + 2) * (2 + 3)$

   fst $(1 + 2, 2 + 3)$

   $(\lambda x \to 1 + x) (2 * 3)$

2. Show why outermost evaluation is preferable to innermost for the purposes of evaluating the expression *fst* $(1 + 2, 2 + 3)$.

3. Given the definition $mult = \lambda x \to (\lambda y \to x * y)$, show how the evaluation of *mult* 3 4 can be broken down into four separate steps.

4. Using a list comprehension, define an expression *fibs* :: [*Integer*] that generates the infinite sequence of Fibonacci numbers

   $0, 1, 1, 2, 3, 5, 8, 13, 21, 34, \cdots$

   using the following simple procedure:

   – the first two numbers are 0 and 1;
   – the next is the sum of the previous two;
   – return to the second step.

   Hint: make use of the library functions *zip* and *tail*. Note that numbers in the Fibonacci sequence quickly become large, hence the use of the type *Integer* of arbitrary-precision integers above.

5. Using *fibs*, define a function *fib* :: *Int* $\to$ *Integer* that returns the nth Fibonnaci number (counting from zero), and an expression that calculates the first Fibonacci number greater than one thousand.

6. Define appropriate versions of the library functions

$$
\begin{aligned}
&repeat && :: && a \to [\,a\,] \\
&repeat\ x && = && xs\ \textbf{where}\ xs = x : xs \\
&take && :: && Int \to [\,a\,] \to [\,a\,] \\
&take\ 0\ \_ && = && [\,] \\
&take\ (n+1)\ [\,] && = && [\,] \\
&take\ (n+1)\ (x : xs) && = && x : take\ n\ xs \\
&replicate && :: && Int \to a \to [\,a\,] \\
&replicate\ n && = && take\ n \circ repeat
\end{aligned}
$$

for the following type of binary trees:

$$\textbf{data}\ Tree\ a\ =\ Leaf \mid Node\ (Tree\ a)\ a\ (Tree\ a)$$

chapter 13

Reasoning about programs

In this final chapter we introduce the idea of reasoning about Haskell programs. We start by reviewing the notion of equational reasoning, then consider how it can be applied in Haskell, introduce the important technique of induction, show how induction can be used to eliminate uses of the append operator, and conclude by proving the correctness of a simple compiler.

13.1 | Equational reasoning

At school we learn basic algebraic properties of numbers, such as the fact that multiplication is commutative, addition is associative, and multiplication distributes over addition on both the left- and right-hand sides:

$$
\begin{aligned}
x\,y &= y\,x \\
x + (y + z) &= (x + y) + z \\
x\,(y + z) &= x\,y + x\,z \\
(x + y)\,z &= x\,z + y\,z
\end{aligned}
$$

For example, using these properties we can show that a product of the form $(x + a)(x + b)$ can be expanded to a summation $x^2 + (a + b)x + a\,b$:

$$
\begin{aligned}
&(x + a)(x + b) \\
=\quad &\{\text{ left distributivity }\} \\
&(x + a)\,x + (x + a)\,b \\
=\quad &\{\text{ right distributivity }\} \\
&x\,x + a\,x + x\,b + a\,b \\
=\quad &\{\text{ squaring }\} \\
&x^2 + a\,x + x\,b + a\,b \\
=\quad &\{\text{ commutativity }\} \\
&x^2 + a\,x + b\,x + a\,b \\
=\quad &\{\text{ right distributivity }\} \\
&x^2 + (a + b)\,x + a\,b
\end{aligned}
$$

Note that in this calculation we follow the common practice of implicitly exploiting associativity properties, in this case the associativity of addition by omitting parentheses when more than one addition is used in sequence.

As well as being interesting in their their own right, algebraic properties can also have a computational significance. For example, the expression $x\,(y+z)$ requires two operations (one multiplication and one addition), whereas the equivalent expression $x\,y+x\,z$ requires three (two multiplications and one addition). Hence even though these two expressions are algebraically equal, in terms of efficiency the former is preferable to the latter.

13.2 | Reasoning about Haskell

The same style of equational reasoning can also be used in Haskell. For example, in this context the equation $x*y=y*x$ means that for any expressions x and y of the same numeric types, evaluation of $x*y$ and $y*x$ will always produce the same numeric value. Note that the equality operator $==$ provided within Haskell itself is not used when stating such properties, as in $x*y == y*x$, because we are aiming to use mathematics as a language to reason about Haskell, rather than using Haskell as a language to reason about itself, which would be somewhat circular.

When reasoning about Haskell, we do not just use properties of built-in operations of the language such as addition and multiplication, but also use the equations from which user-defined functions are constructed. For example, consider the following function that doubles an integer:

$$
\begin{array}{lll}
double & :: & Int \to Int \\
double\ x & = & x + x
\end{array}
$$

As well as being viewed as the definition of a function, this equation can also be viewed as a property that can be used when reasoning about this function. In particular, as a logical property the above equation states that for any integer expression x, the expression $double\ x$ can freely be replaced by $x+x$, and, conversely, that the expression $x+x$ can freely be replaced by $double\ x$. In this manner, when reasoning about programs, function definitions can be both applied from left-to-right and unapplied from right-to-left.

However, some care is required when reasoning about functions that are defined using multiple equations. For example, consider a function that decides if an integer is zero, defined using two equations:

$$
\begin{array}{lll}
isZero & :: & Int \to Bool \\
isZero\ 0 & = & True \\
isZero\ n & = & False
\end{array}
$$

The first equation, $isZero\ 0 = True$, can freely be viewed as a logical property that can be applied in both directions. However, this is not the case for the second equation, $isZero\ n = False$. In particular, because the order in which the equations are written is significant, an expression of the form $isZero\ n$ can only be replaced by $False$ provided that $n \neq 0$, as in the case when $n = 0$ the first equation applies. Dually, it is only valid to unapply the equation *isZero n = False* and replace *False* by an expression of the form *isZero n* in the case when $n \neq 0$, for the same reason.

More generally, when a function is defined using multiple equations, the equations cannot be viewed as logical properties in isolation from one another, but need to be interpreted in light of the order in which patterns are matched within the equations. For this reason, it is preferable to define functions in a manner that does not rely on the order in which their equations are written. For example, if we rewrite the above definition using a guard

$$
\begin{aligned}
isZero\ 0 \quad\quad &=\quad True \\
isZero\ n \mid n \neq 0 \quad &=\quad False
\end{aligned}
$$

then it is now explicitly clear that *isZero n* can only be replaced by *False*, and conversely that *False* can only be replaced by *isZero n*, when the guard $n \neq 0$ is satisfied. Patterns that do not rely on the order in which they are matched are called *disjoint* or *non-overlapping*. In order to simplify the process of reasoning about programs, it is good practice to use non-overlapping patterns whenever possible. For example, most of the functions in the standard library given in appendix A are defined in this manner.

13.3 | Simple examples

As a simple example of equational reasoning in Haskell, recall the following definition of the library function that reverses a list:

$$
\begin{aligned}
reverse \quad\quad\quad &::\quad [a] \to [a] \\
reverse\ [\,] \quad\quad &=\quad [\,] \\
reverse\ (x:xs) \quad &=\quad reverse\ xs \mathbin{+\!\!+} [x]
\end{aligned}
$$

Using this definition, we can show that *reverse* has no effect on singleton lists, in the sense that $reverse\ [x] = [x]$ for any element x:

$$
\begin{aligned}
&reverse\ [x] \\
=\quad &\{\ \text{list notation}\ \} \\
&reverse\ (x:[\,]) \\
=\quad &\{\ \text{applying } reverse\ \} \\
&reverse\ [\,] \mathbin{+\!\!+} [x] \\
=\quad &\{\ \text{applying } reverse\ \} \\
&[\,] \mathbin{+\!\!+} [x] \\
=\quad &\{\ \text{applying } \mathbin{+\!\!+}\ \} \\
&[x]
\end{aligned}
$$

Hence any expression of the form $reverse\ [x]$ in a program can freely be replaced by $[x]$ without change in meaning, but with a change in efficiency by avoiding the need to apply the *reverse* function.

Equational reasoning is often combined with some form of case analysis. For example, consider the logical negation function:

$$
\begin{aligned}
\neg \quad\quad &::\quad Bool \to Bool \\
\neg\ False \quad &=\quad True \\
\neg\ True \quad &=\quad False
\end{aligned}
$$

Because this function is defined by pattern matching, properties of $\neg$ are normally proved by case analysis on its argument. For example, the fact that $\neg$ is its own inverse, $\neg\,(\neg\,b) = b$ for all logical values b, can be shown by case analysis on the two possible values for b. For example, the case when $b = \textit{False}$ is verified below, and $b = \textit{True}$ follows similarly:

$$
\begin{aligned}
& \neg\,(\neg\,\textit{False}) \\
= \quad & \{\text{ applying the inner } \neg \} \\
& \neg\,\textit{True} \\
= \quad & \{\text{ applying } \neg \} \\
& \textit{False}
\end{aligned}
$$

13.4 | Induction on numbers

Most interesting functional programs involve some form of recursion. Reasoning about such programs normally proceeds using the simple but powerful technique of *induction*. Let us begin by recalling the simplest example of a recursive type, namely the type of natural numbers:

$$\textbf{data } \textit{Nat} \;=\; \textit{Zero} \mid \textit{Succ Nat}$$

This declaration states that $\textit{Zero}$ is a value of type $\textit{Nat}$ (the base case), and that if n is a value of type $\textit{Nat}$, then so is $\textit{Succ } n$ (the recursive case). Implicit in the declaration is the fact that $\textit{Zero}$ and $\textit{Succ}$ are the only constructors for the type $\textit{Nat}$. Hence, the values of $\textit{Nat}$ can be enumerated as follows:

$$
\begin{aligned}
& \textit{Zero} \\
& \textit{Succ Zero} \\
& \textit{Succ (Succ Zero)} \\
& \textit{Succ (Succ (Succ Zero))} \\
& \quad\vdots
\end{aligned}
$$

For simplicity, we only consider the finite natural numbers, obtained by starting with $\textit{Zero}$ and applying $\textit{Succ}$ a finite number of times. In particular, we do not consider infinity, defined by $\textit{inf} = \textit{Succ inf}$. A similar comment applies to all the other recursive types that we consider in this chapter.

Now suppose we want to prove that some property, p say, holds for all (finite) natural numbers. Then the principle of induction states that it is sufficient to show that p holds for $\textit{Zero}$, called the *base case*, and that p is preserved by $\textit{Succ}$, called the *inductive case*. More precisely, in the inductive case one is required to show that if the property p holds for any natural number n, called the *induction hypothesis*, then it also holds for $\textit{Succ } n$.

Why is induction sufficient to show that p holds for all natural numbers? For example, how does it then follow that p holds for $\textit{Succ (Succ Zero)}$. Starting from the base case that p holds for $\textit{Zero}$, we can apply the inductive case once to conclude that p holds for $\textit{Succ Zero}$, by taking $n = \textit{Zero}$, and then apply the inductive case a second time to conclude that p holds for $\textit{Succ (Succ Zero)}$, by taking $n = \textit{Succ Zero}$. In a similar manner, it can be established that p holds for any natural number.

It is useful to draw an analogy with the "domino effect". Suppose there is a line of dominoes standing on end and you know that the first domino will fall, and that whenever a domino falls then its next neighbour will also fall. Then it is clear that all the dominoes will fall, by applying the first fact to get the process started, and repeatedly applying the second to keep it going. The same pattern of reasoning occurs with induction: we first verify the required property for *Zero* (the first domino falls), then that the property is preserved by *Succ* (if any domino falls, then so will its neighbour), and conclude that the property holds for all natural numbers (all dominoes fall).

As a concrete example, consider the definition of a recursive function that takes two natural numbers and adds them together:

$$
\begin{aligned}
&add &&:: && Nat \to Nat \to Nat \\
&add\ Zero\ m &&= && m \\
&add\ (Succ\ n)\ m &&= && Succ\ (add\ n\ m)
\end{aligned}
$$

From the first equation it is immediate that $add\ Zero\ m = m$ holds for any natural number m. Now let us show that the dual property, $add\ n\ Zero = n$, which we abbreviate by p, also holds for all natural numbers n. We proceed by induction on n. The base case, showing that $p\ Zero$ holds, amounts to showing that $add\ Zero\ Zero = Zero$, which is immediate:

$$
\begin{aligned}
&\quad add\ Zero\ Zero \\
&= \quad \{\ \text{applying } add\ \} \\
&\quad Zero
\end{aligned}
$$

For the inductive case, we must show that if p holds for any natural number n, then $p\ (Succ\ n)$ also holds. That is, using the induction hypothesis $add\ n\ Zero = n$ as an assumption, we must show that $add\ (Succ\ n)\ Zero = Succ\ n$, which can be verified by the following calculation:

$$
\begin{aligned}
&\quad add\ (Succ\ n)\ Zero \\
&= \quad \{\ \text{applying } add\ \} \\
&\quad Succ\ (add\ n\ Zero) \\
&= \quad \{\ \text{induction hypothesis}\ \} \\
&\quad Succ\ n
\end{aligned}
$$

$$\square$$

Because proofs by induction normally involve more than one calculation, it is useful to explicitly indicate the end of the proof. For this purpose, we use a square box □ in the right-hand margin, as illustrated above.

As another example, let us now show that addition of natural numbers is associative. That is, $add\ x\ (add\ y\ z) = add\ (add\ x\ y)\ z$ for all natural numbers x, y and z. There are three arguments to choose from, so which should induction be performed over? Note that the add function is defined by pattern matching on its first argument, so it is natural to try induction on x, which appears twice as the first argument to add in the associativity equation, whereas y only appears once as such and z never. Using induction on x, the proof of the associativity of add proceeds as follows.

Base case:

$$add\ Zero\ (add\ y\ z)$$
$=$ { applying the outer add }
$$add\ y\ z$$
$=$ { unapplying add }
$$add\ (add\ Zero\ y)\ z$$

Inductive case:

$$add\ (Succ\ x)\ (add\ y\ z)$$
$=$ { applying the outer add }
$$Succ\ (add\ x\ (add\ y\ z))$$
$=$ { induction hypothesis }
$$Succ\ (add\ (add\ x\ y)\ z)$$
$=$ { unapplying the outer add }
$$add\ (Succ\ (add\ x\ y)\ z)$$
$=$ { unapplying the inner add }
$$add\ (add\ (Succ\ x)\ y)\ z$$

$\square$

Note that both cases start by applying definitions, and conclude by unapplying definitions. This pattern is typical in proofs by induction, but the latter part may seem somewhat mysterious at first. In particular, knowing which definitions to unapply seems to require a degree of foresight. In practice, however, if one becomes stuck at a certain point during such a calculation, progress can often be made by focusing on the desired end result and trying to work backwards to the point where one became stuck.

For example, after applying the induction hypothesis in the inductive case above to obtain $Succ\ (add\ (add\ x\ y)\ z)$, it may not be clear how to proceed, as there are no more definitions that can be applied. However, if we then focus on the expression that we are aiming towards, $add\ (add\ (Succ\ x)\ y)\ z$, we can simply apply the inner add and then the outer add to produce the expression at which we became stuck, which process can then be reversed (turning applying into unapplying) to complete the calculation.

Although we have introduced induction using the recursive type Nat, the same principle can also be used with the integers that are built-in to Haskell. In particular, to prove that some property p holds for all integers $n \geq 0$, it is sufficient to show that p holds for 0, the base case, and that if p holds for any $n \geq 0$, then it also holds for $n + 1$, the inductive case.

For example, consider the following definition for the library function $replicate$ that produces a list with n identical elements:

```
replicate          ::  Int → a → [a]
replicate 0 _       =  []
replicate (n + 1) x =  x : replicate n x
```

Then it is easy to show that this function does indeed produce a list with n elements, that is $length\ (replicate\ n\ x) = n$, by induction on $n \geq 0$.

Base case:

$$length \; (replicate \; 0 \; x)$$
$$= \qquad \{ \text{applying } replicate \}$$
$$length \; [\,]$$
$$= \qquad \{ \text{applying } length \}$$
$$0$$

Inductive case:

$$length \; (replicate \; (n + 1) \; x)$$
$$= \qquad \{ \text{applying } replicate \}$$
$$length \; (x : replicate \; n \; x)$$
$$= \qquad \{ \text{applying } length \}$$
$$1 + length \; (replicate \; n \; x)$$
$$= \qquad \{ \text{induction hypothesis} \}$$
$$1 + n$$
$$= \qquad \{ \text{commutativity of } + \}$$
$$n + 1$$

$\square$

13.5 | Induction on lists

Induction is not restricted to natural numbers, but can also be used to reason about other recursive types, such as the type of lists. Just as natural numbers are built up recursively from zero by applying the successor function, so lists are built up from the empty list by applying the cons operator.

Suppose we want to prove that some property p holds for all lists. Then the induction principle for lists states that it is sufficient to show that p holds for the empty list [ ], the base case, and that if p holds for any list xs, then it also holds for $x : xs$ for any element x, the inductive case. Of course, both the element x and the list xs must be of the appropriate types.

As an example, let us show that the function $reverse$ defined earlier in this chapter is its own inverse, $reverse \; (reverse \; xs) = xs$, by induction on xs. The base case is verified simply by applying the definition of $reverse$:

$$reverse \; (reverse \; [\,])$$
$$= \qquad \{ \text{applying the inner } reverse \}$$
$$reverse \; [\,]$$
$$= \qquad \{ \text{applying } reverse \}$$
$$[\,]$$

For the inductive case, using the assumption $reverse \; (reverse \; xs) = xs$, we show that $reverse \; (reverse \; (x : xs)) = x : xs$, as follows:

$$reverse \; (reverse \; (x : xs))$$
$$= \qquad \{ \text{applying the inner } reverse \}$$
$$reverse \; (reverse \; xs \; {+\!\!+} \; [x])$$
$$= \qquad \{ \text{distributivity - see below} \}$$
$$reverse \; [x] \; {+\!\!+} \; reverse \; (reverse \; xs)$$

$$= \quad \{ \text{ singleton lists - see below } \}$$
$$[x] \mathbin{+\!\!+} reverse\ (reverse\ xs)$$
$$= \quad \{ \text{ induction hypothesis } \}$$
$$[x] \mathbin{+\!\!+} xs$$
$$= \quad \{ \text{ applying } \mathbin{+\!\!+} \}$$
$$x : xs$$

$\square$

This calculation uses two auxiliary properties of the function *reverse*, namely our earlier result that *reverse* preserves singleton lists, $reverse\ [x] = [x]$, together with a new result that *reverse* distributes over append, except that the order of the two argument lists is then swapped:

$$reverse\ (xs \mathbin{+\!\!+} ys) \quad = \quad reverse\ ys \mathbin{+\!\!+} reverse\ xs$$

Technically, we say that the distribution is contravariant. Because the append operator $\mathbin{+\!\!+}$ is defined by pattern matching on its first argument, it is natural to attempt to verify this property by induction on xs.

Base case:

$$reverse\ ([\,] \mathbin{+\!\!+} ys)$$
$$= \quad \{ \text{ applying } \mathbin{+\!\!+} \}$$
$$reverse\ ys$$
$$= \quad \{ \text{ property of } \mathbin{+\!\!+}, \text{ see exercise 5 } \}$$
$$reverse\ ys \mathbin{+\!\!+} [\,]$$
$$= \quad \{ \text{ unapplying } reverse \}$$
$$reverse\ ys \mathbin{+\!\!+} reverse\ [\,]$$

Inductive case:

$$reverse\ ((x : xs) \mathbin{+\!\!+} ys)$$
$$= \quad \{ \text{ applying } \mathbin{+\!\!+} \}$$
$$reverse\ (x : (xs \mathbin{+\!\!+} ys))$$
$$= \quad \{ \text{ applying } reverse \}$$
$$reverse\ (xs \mathbin{+\!\!+} ys) \mathbin{+\!\!+} [x]$$
$$= \quad \{ \text{ induction hypothesis } \}$$
$$(reverse\ ys \mathbin{+\!\!+} reverse\ xs) \mathbin{+\!\!+} [x]$$
$$= \quad \{ \text{ associativity of } \mathbin{+\!\!+} \}$$
$$reverse\ ys \mathbin{+\!\!+} (reverse\ xs \mathbin{+\!\!+} [x])$$
$$= \quad \{ \text{ unapplying the second } reverse \}$$
$$reverse\ ys \mathbin{+\!\!+} reverse\ (x : xs)$$

$\square$

This calculation in turn uses the fact that $\mathbin{+\!\!+}$ is associative, which can be verified by induction in a similar manner to our earlier result that *add* is associative (see exercise 5 for this chapter.)

13.6 | Making append vanish

Many recursive functions are naturally defined using the append operator $\mathbin{+\!\!+}$ on lists, but this operator carries a considerable efficiency cost when used recursively. In this section, we show how induction can be used to eliminate such uses of append, and hence make functions more efficient. As a first example, consider again the following definition:

$$
\begin{aligned}
reverse & \quad :: \quad [a] \to [a] \\
reverse\ [] & \quad = \quad [] \\
reverse\ (x : xs) & \quad = \quad reverse\ xs \mathbin{+\!\!+} [x]
\end{aligned}
$$

How efficient is *reverse*? First of all, it is easy to show that the number of reduction steps required to evaluate $xs \mathbin{+\!\!+} ys$ is one greater than the length of xs, assuming for simplicity that both xs and ys are already fully evaluated. As a result, we say that $\mathbin{+\!\!+}$ takes linear time in the length of its first argument. In turn, the number of steps required by *reverse xs* for a list of length n can be shown to be the sum of the integers from 1 to $n + 1$, which is $(n + 1)(n + 2)/2$. Multiplying out the brackets using the equation verified at the start of this chapter gives $(n^2 + 3n + 2)/2$, as a result of which we say that *reverse* takes quadratic time in the length of its argument.

Quadratic time is bad. For example, reversing a list with ten thousand elements will take approximately fifty million reduction steps. Fortunately, however, through the use of induction it is easy to eliminate the use of append in the definition of *reverse*, and hence improve its efficiency.

The trick is to attempt to define a more general function, which combines the behaviours of *reverse* and $\mathbin{+\!\!+}$. In particular, we seek to define a recursive function *reverse'* that satisfies the following equation:

$$
reverse'\ xs\ ys \quad = \quad reverse\ xs \mathbin{+\!\!+} ys
$$

That is, applying *reverse'* to two lists should give the result of reversing the first list, appended together with the second list. If we can define such a function, then *reverse* itself can be redefined by *reverse xs = reverse' xs* [ ], using the fact that the empty list is the identity for append.

Rather the giving the definition for *reverse'*, and then showing that it satisfies the above equation, we can in fact use this equation as the driving force for constructing the definition itself. In particular, we simply attempt to verify this equation by induction on xs. The base case results in an equation that gives the definition for *reverse'* [ ] *ys*, while the inductive case results in an equation that gives the definition for *reverse'* $(x : xs)$ *ys*.

Base case:

$$
\begin{aligned}
& reverse'\ [\ ]\ ys \\
= \quad & \{ \text{ specification of } reverse' \} \\
& reverse\ [\ ] \mathbin{+\!\!+} ys \\
= \quad & \{ \text{ applying } reverse \} \\
& [\ ] \mathbin{+\!\!+} ys \\
= \quad & \{ \text{ applying } \mathbin{+\!\!+} \} \\
& ys
\end{aligned}
$$

Inductive case:

$$
\begin{aligned}
& reverse'\ (x : xs)\ ys \\
= \quad & \{ \text{ specification of } reverse' \}
\end{aligned}
$$

$$reverse\ (x:xs) \mathbin{+\!\!+} ys$$
$$= \qquad \{\ \text{applying } reverse\ \}$$
$$(reverse\ xs \mathbin{+\!\!+} [x]) \mathbin{+\!\!+} ys$$
$$= \qquad \{\ \text{associativity of } \mathbin{+\!\!+}\ \}$$
$$reverse\ xs \mathbin{+\!\!+} ([x] \mathbin{+\!\!+} ys)$$
$$= \qquad \{\ \text{induction hypothesis}\ \}$$
$$reverse'\ xs\ ([x] \mathbin{+\!\!+} ys)$$
$$= \qquad \{\ \text{applying } \mathbin{+\!\!+}\ \}$$
$$reverse'\ xs\ (x:ys)$$

$\square$

We conclude from this proof that the definition

$$
\begin{array}{lcl}
reverse' & :: & [a] \to [a] \to [a] \\
reverse'\ [\,]\ ys & = & ys \\
reverse'\ (x:xs)\ ys & = & reverse'\ xs\ (x:ys)
\end{array}
$$

suffices to show that $reverse'\ xs\ ys = reverse\ xs \mathbin{+\!\!+} ys$ by induction. Note that the definition for $reverse'$ does not refer to the original $reverse$ function, or append. Hence, $reverse$ itself can now be redefined as follows:

$$
\begin{array}{lcl}
reverse & :: & [a] \to [a] \\
reverse\ xs & = & reverse'\ xs\ [\,]
\end{array}
$$

For example, we have:

$$reverse\ [1,2,3]$$
$$= \qquad \{\ \text{applying } reverse\ \}$$
$$reverse'\ [1,2,3]\ [\,]$$
$$= \qquad \{\ \text{applying } reverse'\ \}$$
$$reverse'\ [2,3]\ (1:[\,])$$
$$= \qquad \{\ \text{applying } reverse'\ \}$$
$$reverse'\ [3]\ (2:(1:[\,]))$$
$$= \qquad \{\ \text{applying } reverse'\ \}$$
$$reverse'\ [\,]\ (3:(2:(1:[\,])))$$
$$= \qquad \{\ \text{applying } reverse'\ \}$$
$$3:(2:(1:[\,]))$$

That is, the list is reversed by using an extra argument to accumulate the final result. The new definition for $reverse$ is perhaps less clear than the original version, but it is much more efficient. In particular, the number of reduction steps required to evaluate $reverse\ xs$ for a list of length n using the new definition is simply $n + 2$, and hence $reverse$ now takes linear time in the length of its argument. For example, reversing a list with ten thousand elements will now take approximately ten thousand steps, in contrast to some fifty million with the original definition — quite an improvement!

Note that we have already seen the use of accumulation to improve the efficiency of functions, in the context of the higher-order library function $foldl$ in chapters 7 and 12. For example, the accumulator version of $reverse$ can also be obtained simply by defining $reverse = foldl\ (\lambda xs\ x \to x:xs)\ [\,]$. However, it is instructive to see how the same kind of behaviour can be obtained using induction.

As another example of the elimination of append, which also illustrates the use of induction on trees-like types, consider the following type of binary trees, together with a function that flattens such trees to a list:

$$
\begin{array}{lll}
\textbf{data } \textit{Tree} & = & \textit{Leaf Int} \mid \textit{Node Tree Tree} \\
\textit{flatten} & :: & \textit{Tree} \rightarrow [\textit{Int}] \\
\textit{flatten (Leaf n)} & = & [n] \\
\textit{flatten (Node l r)} & = & \textit{flatten l} \mathbin{+\!\!+} \textit{flatten r}
\end{array}
$$

Because of the use of append, the function *flatten* is inefficient. Let us now construct a more efficient version, by using the same trick as for *reverse*. That is, we seek to define a more general function, *flatten'*, that combines the behaviours of the functions *flatten* and $+\!\!+$:

$$
\textit{flatten' t ns} \quad = \quad \textit{flatten t} \mathbin{+\!\!+} \textit{ns}
$$

In order to prove that some property holds for all trees, the induction principle for the type *Tree* states that it is sufficient to show that it holds for all trees of the form *Leaf n*, and that if the property holds for any trees *l* and *r*, then it also holds for *Node l r*. Using this principle, we construct a definition for *flatten'* that satisfies the above equation as follows.

Base case:

$$
\begin{array}{ll}
& \textit{flatten' (Leaf n) ns} \\
= & \{ \text{ specification of } \textit{flatten' } \} \\
& \textit{flatten (Leaf n)} \mathbin{+\!\!+} \textit{ns} \\
= & \{ \text{ applying } \textit{flatten } \} \\
& [n] \mathbin{+\!\!+} \textit{ns} \\
= & \{ \text{ applying } +\!\!+ \} \\
& n : ns
\end{array}
$$

Inductive case:

$$
\begin{array}{ll}
& \textit{flatten' (Node l r) ns} \\
= & \{ \text{ specification of } \textit{flatten' } \} \\
& (\textit{flatten l} \mathbin{+\!\!+} \textit{flatten r}) \mathbin{+\!\!+} \textit{ns} \\
= & \{ \text{ associativity of } +\!\!+ \} \\
& \textit{flatten l} \mathbin{+\!\!+} (\textit{flatten r} \mathbin{+\!\!+} \textit{ns}) \\
= & \{ \text{ induction hypothesis for } l \} \\
& \textit{flatten' l} (\textit{flatten r} \mathbin{+\!\!+} \textit{ns}) \\
= & \{ \text{ induction hypothesis for } r \} \\
& \textit{flatten' l} (\textit{flatten' r ns})
\end{array}
$$

$\square$

We conclude that the definition

$$
\begin{array}{lll}
\textit{flatten'} & :: & \textit{Tree} \rightarrow [\textit{Int}] \rightarrow [\textit{Int}] \\
\textit{flatten' (Leaf n) ns} & = & n : ns \\
\textit{flatten' (Node l r) ns} & = & \textit{flatten' l} (\textit{flatten' r ns})
\end{array}
$$

satisfies the specification for *flatten'*, and hence that the original function *flatten* can now be redefined as follows:

$$
\begin{array}{lll}
flatten & :: & Tree \to [\,Int\,] \\
flatten\ t & = & flatten'\ t\ [\,] \\
\end{array}
$$

Once again, the new definition for *flatten* is perhaps less clear than the original version, but is much more efficient, by using an extra argument to accumulate the final result, rather than using append.

13.7 | Compiler correctness

We conclude this chapter with an extended example. Recall that in chapter 10 we defined a type of arithmetic expressions built up from integers using an addition operator, together with a function (here called *eval*) that evaluates an expression directly to an integer value:

$$
\begin{array}{lll}
\textbf{data}\ Expr & = & Val\ Int \mid Add\ Expr\ Expr \\
eval & :: & Expr \to Int \\
eval\ (Val\ n) & = & n \\
eval\ (Add\ x\ y) & = & eval\ x + eval\ y \\
\end{array}
$$

Such expressions can also be evaluated indirectly, by means of code that executes using a stack. In this context, a stack is simply a list of integers, and code comprises a list of push and add operations on the stack:

$$
\begin{array}{lll}
\textbf{type}\ Stack & = & [\,Int\,] \\
\textbf{type}\ Code & = & [\,Op\,] \\
\textbf{data}\ Op & = & PUSH\ Int \mid ADD \\
\end{array}
$$

The meaning of such code is given by defining a function that executes a piece of code using an initial stack to give a final stack:

$$
\begin{array}{lll}
exec & :: & Code \to Stack \to Stack \\
exec\ [\,]\ s & = & s \\
exec\ (PUSH\ n : c)\ s & = & exec\ c\ (n : s) \\
exec\ (ADD : c)\ (m : n : s) & = & exec\ c\ (n + m : s) \\
\end{array}
$$

That is, the push operation places a new integer on the top of the stack, while add replaces the top two integers by their sum. Using these operations, it is now straightforward to define a function that compiles an expression into code. An integer value is compiled by simply pushing that value, while an addition is compiled by first compiling the two argument expressions x and y, and then adding the resulting two integers on the stack:

$$
\begin{array}{lll}
comp & :: & Expr \to Code \\
comp\ (Val\ n) & = & [\,PUSH\ n\,] \\
comp\ (Add\ x\ y) & = & comp\ x \mathbin{+\!\!+} comp\ y \mathbin{+\!\!+} [\,ADD\,] \\
\end{array}
$$

Note that when an add operation is performed, the value of expression y will be the top of the stack, and the value of x will be the second top, hence the swapping of these two values in the definition of *exec*.

To illustrate the behaviour of the three functions defined above, if $e :: Expr$ represents the expression $(2 + 3) + 4$, then we have:

> *eval e*

9

> *comp e*

$[PUSH\ 2, PUSH\ 3, ADD, PUSH\ 4, ADD]$

> *exec* (*comp e*) [ ]

[9]

Generalising from this example, the correctness of our compiler for expressions can be expressed by the following equation:

$$exec\ (comp\ e)\ [\ ] \quad = \quad [eval\ e]$$

That is, compiling an expression and then executing the resulting code using an empty initial stack gives the same final stack as evaluating the expression and then converting the resulting integer into a singleton stack. For the purposes of proving this result, however, we will see that it is necessary to generalise from the empty initial stack to an arbitrary initial stack:

$$exec\ (comp\ e)\ s \quad = \quad eval\ e : s$$

Using induction for the type *Expr*, which is the same as induction for the type *Tree* in the previous section except that the names of the constructors are different, the compiler correctness equation can be verified as follows.

Base case:

$exec\ (comp\ (Val\ n))\ s$

$=$ { applying *comp* }

$exec\ [PUSH\ n]\ s$

$=$ { applying *exec* }

$n : s$

$=$ { unapplying *eval* }

$eval\ (Val\ n) : s$

Inductive case:

$exec\ (comp\ (Add\ x\ y))\ s$

$=$ { applying *comp* }

$exec\ (comp\ x \mathbin{+\!\!+} comp\ y \mathbin{+\!\!+} [ADD])\ s$

$=$ { associativity of $\mathbin{+\!\!+}$ }

$exec\ (comp\ x \mathbin{+\!\!+} (comp\ y \mathbin{+\!\!+} [ADD]))\ s$

$=$ { distributivity - see below }

$exec\ (comp\ y \mathbin{+\!\!+} [ADD])\ (exec\ (comp\ x)\ s)$

$=$ { induction hypothesis for x }

$exec\ (comp\ y \mathbin{+\!\!+} [ADD])\ (eval\ x : s)$

$=$ { distributivity again }

$exec\ [ADD]\ (exec\ (comp\ y)\ (eval\ x : s))$

$=$ { induction hypothesis for y }

$$exec\ [ADD]\ (eval\ y : eval\ x : s)$$
$$=\quad \{\ \text{applying}\ exec\ \}$$
$$(eval\ x + eval\ y) : s$$
$$=\quad \{\ \text{unapplying}\ eval\ \}$$
$$eval\ (Add\ x\ y) : s$$

□

Note that without having generalised the result to an arbitrary stack, the second induction hypothesis step would not be applicable, because the stack becomes non-empty at this point. The distributivity property used in the inductive case states that executing two pieces of code appended together gives the same result as executing the two pieces of code in sequence:

$$exec\ (c \mathbin{+\!\!+} d)\ s\quad =\quad exec\ d\ (exec\ c\ s)$$

The proof of this property proceeds by induction on the code c, with the inductive case being split into two separate cases, depending upon whether the first operation in the code is a push or an addition.

Base case:

$$exec\ ([\ ] \mathbin{+\!\!+} d)\ s$$
$$=\quad \{\ \text{applying}\ \mathbin{+\!\!+}\ \}$$
$$exec\ d\ s$$
$$=\quad \{\ \text{unapplying}\ exec\ \}$$
$$exec\ d\ (exec\ [\ ]\ s)$$

Inductive case:

$$exec\ ((PUSH\ n : c) \mathbin{+\!\!+} d)\ s$$
$$=\quad \{\ \text{applying}\ \mathbin{+\!\!+}\ \}$$
$$exec\ (PUSH\ n : (c \mathbin{+\!\!+} d))\ s$$
$$=\quad \{\ \text{applying}\ exec\ \}$$
$$exec\ (c \mathbin{+\!\!+} d)\ (n : s)$$
$$=\quad \{\ \text{induction hypothesis}\ \}$$
$$exec\ d\ (exec\ c\ (n : s))$$
$$=\quad \{\ \text{unapplying}\ exec\ \}$$
$$exec\ d\ (exec\ (PUSH\ n : c)\ s)$$

Inductive case:

$$exec\ ((ADD : c) \mathbin{+\!\!+} d)\ s$$
$$=\quad \{\ \text{applying}\ \mathbin{+\!\!+}\ \}$$
$$exec\ (ADD : (c \mathbin{+\!\!+} d))\ s$$
$$=\quad \{\ \text{assume}\ s\ \text{of the form}\ m : n : s'\ \}$$
$$exec\ (ADD : (c \mathbin{+\!\!+} d))\ (m : n : s')$$
$$=\quad \{\ \text{applying}\ exec\ \}$$
$$exec\ (c \mathbin{+\!\!+} d)\ (n + m : s')$$
$$=\quad \{\ \text{induction hypothesis}\ \}$$
$$exec\ d\ (exec\ c\ (n + m : s'))$$
$$=\quad \{\ \text{unapplying}\ exec\ \}$$
$$exec\ d\ (exec\ (ADD : c)\ (m : n : s'))$$

□

The stack not having the assumed form in the second inductive case corresponds to a stack underflow error. In practice, this will never arise, because the structure of the compiler ensures that the stack will always contain at least two integers when an add operation is performed.

In fact, however, both the distributivity property and its consequent underflow issue can be avoided altogether by applying the technique of the previous section to eliminate the use of append. In particular, we seek to define a generalised function $comp'$ with the following property:

$$comp' \ e \ c \ = \ comp \ e \mathbin{+\!\!+} c$$

By induction on e, we can construct the definition

$$
\begin{array}{lll}
comp' & :: & Expr \to Code \to Code \\
comp' \ (Val \ n) \ c & = & PUSH \ n : c \\
comp' \ (Add \ x \ y) \ c & = & comp' \ x \ (comp' \ y \ (ADD : c))
\end{array}
$$

from which it follows that we can recover our original definition by $comp \ e = comp' \ e \ [\,]$. In turn, the correctness of the new version of the compiler with respect to our semantics can now be stated as follows:

$$exec \ (comp' \ e \ c) \ s \ = \ exec \ c \ (eval \ e : s)$$

That is, compiling an expression and then executing the resulting code together with arbitrary additional code gives the same result as executing the additional code with the value of the expression on top of the original stack. The proof of this result is by induction on the expression e.

Base case:

$$
\begin{array}{ll}
& exec \ (comp' \ (Val \ n) \ c) \ s \\
= & \{ \ \text{applying} \ comp' \ \} \\
& exec \ (PUSH \ n : c) \ s \\
= & \{ \ \text{applying} \ exec \ \} \\
& exec \ c \ (n : s) \\
= & \{ \ \text{unapplying} \ eval \ \} \\
& exec \ c \ (eval \ (Val \ n) : s)
\end{array}
$$

Inductive case:

$$
\begin{array}{ll}
& exec \ (comp' \ (Add \ x \ y) \ c) \ s \\
= & \{ \ \text{applying} \ comp' \ \} \\
& exec \ (comp' \ x \ (comp' \ y \ (ADD : c))) \ s \\
= & \{ \ \text{induction hypothesis for} \ x \ \} \\
& exec \ (comp' \ y \ (ADD : c)) \ (eval \ x : s) \\
= & \{ \ \text{induction hypothesis for} \ y \ \} \\
& exec \ (ADD : c) \ (eval \ y : eval \ x : s) \\
= & \{ \ \text{applying} \ exec \ \} \\
& exec \ c \ ((eval \ x + eval \ y) : s) \\
= & \{ \ \text{unapplying} \ eval \ \} \\
& exec \ c \ (eval \ (Add \ x \ y) : s)
\end{array}
$$

□

Note that with $s = c = [\,]$, this new result simplifies to $exec\ (comp\ e)\ [\,] = [eval\ e]$, our original statement of correctness. In addition to avoiding the problem of stack underflow in the correctness proof, the accumulator version of the compiler has two further benefits. First of all, it avoids the use of $+\!\!+$, and is hence more efficient. And, secondly, the new proof is less than half the combined length of our previous two proofs. As is often the case in formal reasoning, generalising a result in the appropriate manner can considerably simplify its proof. Mathematics is an excellent tool for guiding the development of efficient programs with simple proofs!

13.8 | Chapter remarks

Reasoning about functional programs is a subject for a book in its own right, and we have only touched the surface here. Topics for further reading include reasoning about partial and infinite structures (5; 8), relational and point-free approaches (1), automated testing of properties (4), reasoning about effects (24), and techniques that avoid induction (14). The compiler example is adapted from (18), and the phrase "making append vanish" is inspired by (30).

13.9 | Exercises

1. Give an example of a function from the standard library in appendix A that is defined using overlapping patterns.

2. Show that $add\ n\ (Succ\ m) = Succ\ (add\ n\ m)$, by induction on n.

3. Using this property, together with $add\ n\ Zero = n$, show that addition is commutative, $add\ n\ m = add\ m\ n$, by induction on n.

4. Using the following definition for the library function that decides if *all* elements of a list satisfy a predicate

$$
\begin{aligned}
all\ p\ [\,] &=& True \\
all\ p\ (x:xs) &=& p\ x \land all\ p\ xs
\end{aligned}
$$

complete the proof of the correctness of *replicate* by showing that it produces a list with identical elements, $all\ (== x)\ (replicate\ n\ x)$, by induction on $n \geq 0$. Hint: show that the property is always *True*.

5. Using the definition

$$
\begin{aligned}
[\,] +\!\!+ ys &=& ys \\
(x:xs) +\!\!+ ys &=& x:(xs +\!\!+ ys)
\end{aligned}
$$

verify the following two properties, by induction on xs:

$$
\begin{aligned}
xs +\!\!+ [\,] &=& xs \\
xs +\!\!+ (ys +\!\!+ zs) &=& (xs +\!\!+ ys) +\!\!+ zs
\end{aligned}
$$

Hint: the proofs are similar to those for the *add* function.

6. The equation *reverse* (*reverse xs*) = *xs* can also be proved using a single auxiliary result, *reverse* (*xs* ++ [*x*]) = *x* : *reverse xs*, which can itself be verified by induction on *xs*. Why might the proof using three auxiliary results as in this chapter be viewed as preferable?

7. Using the definitions

$$
\begin{aligned}
map\ f\ [] &=& [] \\
map\ f\ (x : xs) &=& f\ x : map\ f\ xs \\
(f \circ g)\ x &=& f\ (g\ x)
\end{aligned}
$$

show that *map f* (*map g xs*) = *map* (*f* ∘ *g*) *xs*, by induction on *xs*.

8. Using the definition for ++ given above, together with

$$
\begin{aligned}
take\ 0\ \_ &=& [] \\
take\ (n+1)\ [] &=& [] \\
take\ (n+1)\ (x : xs) &=& x : take\ n\ xs \\
drop\ 0\ xs &=& xs \\
drop\ (n+1)\ [] &=& [] \\
drop\ (n+1)\ (\_ : xs) &=& drop\ n\ xs
\end{aligned}
$$

show that *take n xs* ++ *drop n xs* = *xs*, by simultaneous induction on the integer *n* ≥ 0 and the list *xs*. Hint: there are three cases, one for each pattern of arguments in the definitions of *take* and *drop*.

9. Given the type declaration

data *Tree* = *Leaf Int* | *Node Tree Tree*

show that the number of leaves in a such a tree is always one greater than the number of nodes, by induction on trees. Hint: start by defining functions that count the number of leaves and nodes in a tree.

10. Given the equation *comp' e c* = *comp e* ++ *c*, show how to construct the recursive definition for *comp'*, by induction on *e*.

Appendix A

Standard prelude

In this appendix we present some of the most commonly used definitions from the standard prelude. For clarity, a number of the definitions have been simplified or modified from those given in the Haskell Report (25).

A.1 | Classes

Equality types:

```
class Eq a where
    (==), (≠)            ::  a → a → Bool

    x ≠ y                =  ¬ (x == y)
```

Ordered types:

```
class Eq a ⇒ Ord a where
    (<), (≤), (>), (≥)   ::  a → a → Bool
    min, max             ::  a → a → a

    min x y | x ≤ y      =  x
            | otherwise  =  y
    max x y | x ≤ y      =  y
            | otherwise  =  x
```

Showable types:

```
class Show a where
    show                 ::  a → String
```

Readable types:

```
class Read a where
    read                 ::  String → a
```

Numeric types:

> **class** $(Eq\ a,\ Show\ a) \Rightarrow Num\ a$ **where**
> $(+), (-), (*)$ $::\ a \to a \to a$
> $negate,\ abs,\ signum$ $::\ a \to a$

Integral types:

> **class** $Num\ a \Rightarrow Integral\ a$ **where**
> $div,\ mod$ $::\ a \to a \to a$

Fractional types:

> **class** $Num\ a \Rightarrow Fractional\ a$ **where**
> $(/)$ $::\ a \to a \to a$
> $recip$ $::\ a \to a$
>
> $recip\ n$ $=\ 1\ /\ n$

Monadic types:

> **class** $Monad\ m$ **where**
> $return$ $::\ a \to m\ a$
> $(\!\!>\!\!\!>\!\!=\!)$ $::\ m\ a \to (a \to m\ b) \to m\ b$

A.2 | Logical values

Type declaration:

> **data** $Bool$ $=\ False\ |\ True$
>   **deriving** $(Eq,\ Ord,\ Show,\ Read)$

Logical conjunction:

> $(\wedge)$ $::\ Bool \to Bool \to Bool$
> $False \wedge \_$ $=\ False$
> $True \wedge b$ $=\ b$

Logical disjunction:

> $(\vee)$ $::\ Bool \to Bool \to Bool$
> $False \vee b$ $=\ b$
> $True \vee \_$ $=\ True$

Logical negation:

> $\neg$ $::\ Bool \to Bool$
> $\neg\ False$ $=\ True$
> $\neg\ True$ $=\ False$

Guard that always succeeds:

> $otherwise$ $::\ Bool$
> $otherwise$ $=\ True$

A.3 | Characters and strings

Type declarations:

data *Char* = ···
        deriving (*Eq*, *Ord*, *Show*, *Read*)

type *String* = [*Char*]

Decide if a character is a lower-case letter:

isLower :: *Char* → *Bool*
isLower c = $c \geq$ 'a' $\wedge c \leq$ 'z'

Decide if a character is an upper-case letter:

isUpper :: *Char* → *Bool*
isUpper c = $c \geq$ 'A' $\wedge c \leq$ 'Z'

Decide if a character is alphabetic:

isAlpha :: *Char* → *Bool*
isAlpha c = *isLower c* $\vee$ *isUpper c*

Decide if a character is a digit:

isDigit :: *Char* → *Bool*
isDigit c = $c \geq$ '0' $\wedge c \leq$ '9'

Decide if a character is alpha-numeric:

isAlphaNum :: *Char* → *Bool*
isAlphaNum c = *isAlpha c* $\vee$ *isDigit c*

Decide if a character is spacing:

isSpace :: *Char* → *Bool*
isSpace c = *elem c* " \t\n"

Convert a character to a Unicode number:

ord :: *Char* → *Int*
ord c = ···

Convert a Unicode number to a character:

chr :: *Int* → *Char*
chr n = ···

Convert a digit to an integer:

digitToInt :: *Char* → *Int*
digitToInt c | *isDigit c* = *ord c* − *ord* '0'

Convert an integer to a digit:

$$
\begin{aligned}
&intToDigit &&:: \quad Int \rightarrow Char \\
&intToDigit\ n \\
&\quad |\ n \geq 0 \wedge n \leq 9 &&= \quad chr\ (ord\ '0' + n)
\end{aligned}
$$

Convert a letter to lower-case:

$$
\begin{aligned}
&toLower &&:: \quad Char \rightarrow Char \\
&toLower\ c\ |\ isUpper\ c &&= \quad chr\ (ord\ c - ord\ 'A' + ord\ 'a') \\
&\qquad\qquad\ |\ otherwise &&= \quad c
\end{aligned}
$$

Convert a letter to upper-case:

$$
\begin{aligned}
&toUpper &&:: \quad Char \rightarrow Char \\
&toUpper\ c\ |\ isLower\ c &&= \quad chr\ (ord\ c - ord\ 'a' + ord\ 'A') \\
&\qquad\qquad\ |\ otherwise &&= \quad c
\end{aligned}
$$

A.4 | Numbers

Type declarations:

$$
\begin{aligned}
&\textbf{data}\ Int &&= \quad \cdots \\
&&&\textbf{deriving}\ (Eq,\ Ord,\ Show,\ Read, \\
&&&\qquad\qquad\qquad Num,\ Integral)
\end{aligned}
$$

$$
\begin{aligned}
&\textbf{data}\ Integer &&= \quad \cdots \\
&&&\textbf{deriving}\ (Eq,\ Ord,\ Show,\ Read, \\
&&&\qquad\qquad\qquad Num,\ Integral)
\end{aligned}
$$

$$
\begin{aligned}
&\textbf{data}\ Float &&= \quad \cdots \\
&&&\textbf{deriving}\ (Eq,\ Ord,\ Show,\ Read, \\
&&&\qquad\qquad\qquad Num,\ Fractional)
\end{aligned}
$$

Decide if an integer is even:

$$
\begin{aligned}
&even &&:: \quad Integral\ a \Rightarrow a \rightarrow Bool \\
&even\ n &&= \quad n\ `mod`\ 2 == 0
\end{aligned}
$$

Decide if an integer is odd:

$$
\begin{aligned}
&odd &&:: \quad Integral\ a \Rightarrow a \rightarrow Bool \\
&odd &&= \quad \neg \circ even
\end{aligned}
$$

Exponentiation:

$$
\begin{aligned}
&(\uparrow) &&:: \quad (Num\ a,\ Integral\ b) \Rightarrow a \rightarrow b \rightarrow a \\
&\_ \uparrow 0 &&= \quad 1 \\
&x \uparrow (n+1) &&= \quad x * (x \uparrow n)
\end{aligned}
$$

A.5 | Tuples

Type declarations:

data ()   = $\cdots$
                                    deriving (Eq, Ord, $Show$, $Read$)

data (a, b) = $\cdots$
                                    deriving (Eq, Ord, $Show$, $Read$)

data (a, b, c) = $\cdots$
                                    deriving (Eq, Ord, $Show$, $Read$)

$\vdots$

Select the first component of a pair:

fst :: $(a, b) \rightarrow a$
$fst\ (x, \_)$ = x

Select the second component of a pair:

snd :: $(a, b) \rightarrow b$
$snd\ (\_, y)$ = y

A.6 | Maybe

Type declaration:

data $Maybe\ a$ = $Nothing \mid Just\ a$
                                    deriving (Eq, Ord, $Show$, $Read$)

A.7 | Lists

Type declaration:

data $[a]$ = $[\ ] \mid a : [a]$
                                    deriving (Eq, Ord, $Show$, $Read$)

Decide if a list is empty:

$null$ :: $[a] \rightarrow Bool$
$null\ [\ ]$ = $True$
$null\ (\_ : \_)$ = $False$

Decide if a value is an element of a list:

$elem$ :: $Eq\ a \Rightarrow a \rightarrow [a] \rightarrow Bool$
$elem\ x\ xs$ = $any\ (== x)\ xs$

Decide if all logical values in a list are $True$:

and :: $[Bool] \rightarrow Bool$

$$and \qquad\qquad = \quad foldr\ (\wedge)\ True$$

Decide if any logical value in a list is *True*:

$$or \qquad\qquad :: \quad [Bool] \rightarrow Bool$$
$$or \qquad\qquad = \quad foldr\ (\vee)\ False$$

Decide if all elements of a list satisfy a predicate:

$$all \qquad\qquad :: \quad (a \rightarrow Bool) \rightarrow [a] \rightarrow Bool$$
$$all\ p \qquad\qquad = \quad and \circ map\ p$$

Decide if any element of a list satisfies a predicate:

$$any \qquad\qquad :: \quad (a \rightarrow Bool) \rightarrow [a] \rightarrow Bool$$
$$any\ p \qquad\qquad = \quad or \circ map\ p$$

Select the first element of a non-empty list:

$$head \qquad\qquad :: \quad [a] \rightarrow a$$
$$head\ (x : \_) \qquad\qquad = \quad x$$

Select the last element of a non-empty list:

$$last \qquad\qquad :: \quad [a] \rightarrow a$$
$$last\ [x] \qquad\qquad = \quad x$$
$$last\ (\_ : xs) \qquad\qquad = \quad last\ xs$$

Select the nth element of a non-empty list:

$$(!!) \qquad\qquad :: \quad [a] \rightarrow Int \rightarrow a$$
$$(x : \_)\ !!\ 0 \qquad\qquad = \quad x$$
$$(\_ : xs)\ !!\ (n + 1) \qquad\qquad = \quad xs\ !!\ n$$

Select the first n elements of a list:

$$take \qquad\qquad :: \quad Int \rightarrow [a] \rightarrow [a]$$
$$take\ 0\ \_ \qquad\qquad = \quad [\,]$$
$$take\ (n + 1)\ [\,] \qquad\qquad = \quad [\,]$$
$$take\ (n + 1)\ (x : xs) \qquad\qquad = \quad x : take\ n\ xs$$

Select all elements of a list that satisfy a predicate:

$$filter \qquad\qquad :: \quad (a \rightarrow Bool) \rightarrow [a] \rightarrow [a]$$
$$filter\ p\ xs \qquad\qquad = \quad [x \mid x \leftarrow xs, p\ x]$$

Select elements of a list while they satisfy a predicate:

$$takeWhile \qquad\qquad :: \quad (a \rightarrow Bool) \rightarrow [a] \rightarrow [a]$$
$$takeWhile\ \_\ [\,] \qquad\qquad = \quad [\,]$$
$$takeWhile\ p\ (x : xs)$$
$$\qquad |\ p\ x \qquad\qquad = \quad x : takeWhile\ p\ xs$$
$$\qquad |\ otherwise \qquad\qquad = \quad [\,]$$

Remove the first element from a non-empty list:

$$tail \qquad\qquad :: \quad [a] \rightarrow [a]$$

$$tail \ (\_ : xs) \qquad\qquad = \ xs$$

Remove the last element from a non-empty list:

$$
\begin{aligned}
init & \qquad :: \ [a] \to [a] \\
init \ [\_] & \qquad = \ [] \\
init \ (x : xs) & \qquad = \ x : init \ xs
\end{aligned}
$$

Remove the first n elements from a list:

$$
\begin{aligned}
drop & \qquad :: \ Int \to [a] \to [a] \\
drop \ 0 \ xs & \qquad = \ xs \\
drop \ (n+1) \ [] & \qquad = \ [] \\
drop \ (n+1) \ (\_ : xs) & \qquad = \ drop \ n \ xs
\end{aligned}
$$

Remove elements from a list while they satisfy a predicate:

$$
\begin{aligned}
dropWhile & \qquad :: \ (a \to Bool) \to [a] \to [a] \\
dropWhile \ \_ \ [] & \qquad = \ [] \\
dropWhile \ p \ (x : xs) & \\
\quad | \ p \ x & \qquad = \ dropWhile \ p \ xs \\
\quad | \ otherwise & \qquad = \ x : xs
\end{aligned}
$$

Split a list at the nth element:

$$
\begin{aligned}
splitAt & \qquad :: \ Int \to [a] \to ([a],[a]) \\
splitAt \ n \ xs & \qquad = \ (take \ n \ xs, \ drop \ n \ xs)
\end{aligned}
$$

Split a list using a predicate:

$$
\begin{aligned}
span & \qquad :: \ (a \to Bool) \to [a] \to ([a],[a]) \\
span \ p \ xs & \qquad = \ (takeWhile \ p \ xs, \ dropWhile \ p \ xs)
\end{aligned}
$$

Process a list using an operator that associates to the right:

$$
\begin{aligned}
foldr & \qquad :: \ (a \to b \to b) \to b \to [a] \to b \\
foldr \ \_ \ v \ [] & \qquad = \ v \\
foldr \ f \ v \ (x : xs) & \qquad = \ f \ x \ (foldr \ f \ v \ xs)
\end{aligned}
$$

Process a non-empty list using an operator that associates to the right:

$$
\begin{aligned}
foldr1 & \qquad :: \ (a \to a \to a) \to [a] \to a \\
foldr1 \ \_ \ [x] & \qquad = \ x \\
foldr1 \ f \ (x : xs) & \qquad = \ f \ x \ (foldr1 \ f \ xs)
\end{aligned}
$$

Process a list using an operator that associates to the left:

$$
\begin{aligned}
foldl & \qquad :: \ (a \to b \to a) \to a \to [b] \to a \\
foldl \ \_ \ v \ [] & \qquad = \ v \\
foldl \ f \ v \ (x : xs) & \qquad = \ foldl \ f \ (f \ v \ x) \ xs
\end{aligned}
$$

Process a non-empty list using an operator that associates to the left:

$$
\begin{aligned}
foldl1 & \qquad :: \ (a \to a \to a) \to [a] \to a \\
foldl1 \ f \ (x : xs) & \qquad = \ foldl \ f \ x \ xs
\end{aligned}
$$

Produce an infinite list of identical elements:

$$
\begin{aligned}
&repeat && :: && a \rightarrow [a] \\
&repeat\ x && = && xs\ \textbf{where}\ xs = x : xs
\end{aligned}
$$

Produce a list with n identical elements:

$$
\begin{aligned}
&replicate && :: && Int \rightarrow a \rightarrow [a] \\
&replicate\ n && = && take\ n \circ repeat
\end{aligned}
$$

Produce an infinite list by iterating a function over a value:

$$
\begin{aligned}
&iterate && :: && (a \rightarrow a) \rightarrow a \rightarrow [a] \\
&iterate\ f\ x && = && x : iterate\ f\ (f\ x)
\end{aligned}
$$

Produce a list of pairs from a pair of lists:

$$
\begin{aligned}
&zip && :: && [a] \rightarrow [b] \rightarrow [(a, b)] \\
&zip\ [\,]\ \_ && = && [\,] \\
&zip\ \_\ [\,] && = && [\,] \\
&zip\ (x : xs)\ (y : ys) && = && (x, y) : zip\ xs\ ys
\end{aligned}
$$

Calculate the length of a list:

$$
\begin{aligned}
&length && :: && [a] \rightarrow Int \\
&length && = && foldl\ (\lambda n\ \_ \rightarrow n + 1)\ 0
\end{aligned}
$$

Calculate the sum of a list of numbers:

$$
\begin{aligned}
&sum && :: && Num\ a \Rightarrow [a] \rightarrow a \\
&sum && = && foldl\ (+)\ 0
\end{aligned}
$$

Calculate the product of a list of numbers:

$$
\begin{aligned}
&product && :: && Num\ a \Rightarrow [a] \rightarrow a \\
&product && = && foldl\ (*)\ 1
\end{aligned}
$$

Calculate the minimum of a non-empty list:

$$
\begin{aligned}
&minimum && :: && Ord\ a \Rightarrow [a] \rightarrow a \\
&minimum && = && foldl1\ min
\end{aligned}
$$

Calculate the maximum of a non-empty list:

$$
\begin{aligned}
&maximum && :: && Ord\ a \Rightarrow [a] \rightarrow a \\
&maximum && = && foldl1\ max
\end{aligned}
$$

Append two lists:

$$
\begin{aligned}
&(+\!\!+) && :: && [a] \rightarrow [a] \rightarrow [a] \\
&[\,] +\!\!+ ys && = && ys \\
&(x : xs) +\!\!+ ys && = && x : (xs +\!\!+ ys)
\end{aligned}
$$

Concatenate a list of lists:

$$
\begin{aligned}
&concat && :: && [[a]] \rightarrow [a] \\
&concat && = && foldr\ (+\!\!+)\ [\,]
\end{aligned}
$$

Reverse a list:

$$reverse \qquad\qquad :: \quad [a] \to [a]$$
$$reverse \qquad\qquad = \quad foldl\ (\lambda xs\ x \to x : xs)\ [\,]$$

Apply a function to all elements of a list:

$$map \qquad\qquad :: \quad (a \to b) \to [a] \to [b]$$
$$map\ f\ xs \qquad\qquad = \quad [f\ x \mid x \leftarrow xs]$$

A.8 | Functions

Type declaration:

$$\textbf{data}\ a \to b \qquad\qquad = \quad \cdots$$

Identity function:

$$id \qquad\qquad :: \quad a \to a$$
$$id \qquad\qquad = \quad \lambda x \to x$$

Function composition:

$$(\circ) \qquad\qquad :: \quad (b \to c) \to (a \to b) \to (a \to c)$$
$$f \circ g \qquad\qquad = \quad \lambda x \to f\ (g\ x)$$

Constant functions:

$$const \qquad\qquad :: \quad a \to (b \to a)$$
$$const\ x \qquad\qquad = \quad \lambda\_ \to x$$

Strict application:

$$(\$!) \qquad\qquad :: \quad (a \to b) \to a \to b$$
$$f\ \$!\ x \qquad\qquad = \quad \cdots$$

Convert a function on pairs to a curried function:

$$curry \qquad\qquad :: \quad ((a, b) \to c) \to (a \to b \to c)$$
$$curry\ f \qquad\qquad = \quad \lambda x\ y \to f\ (x, y)$$

Convert a curried function to a function on pairs:

$$uncurry \qquad\qquad :: \quad (a \to b \to c) \to ((a, b) \to c)$$
$$uncurry\ f \qquad\qquad = \quad \lambda(x, y) \to f\ x\ y$$

A.9 | Input/output

Type declaration:

$$\textbf{data}\ IO\ a \qquad\qquad = \quad \cdots$$

Read a character from the keyboard:

$$getChar \qquad :: \quad IO \; Char$$
$$getChar \qquad = \quad \dots$$

Read a string from the keyboard:

$$
\begin{aligned}
getLine \quad &:: \quad IO \; String \\
getLine \quad &= \quad \textbf{do } x \leftarrow getChar \\
&\qquad \textbf{if } x == \text{'\textbackslash n'} \textbf{ then} \\
&\qquad\qquad return \text{ ""} \\
&\qquad \textbf{else} \\
&\qquad\qquad \textbf{do } xs \leftarrow getLine \\
&\qquad\qquad return \; (x : xs)
\end{aligned}
$$

Read a value from the keyboard:

$$
\begin{aligned}
readLn \quad &:: \quad Read \; a \Rightarrow IO \; a \\
readLn \quad &= \quad \textbf{do } xs \leftarrow getLine \\
&\qquad return \; (read \; xs)
\end{aligned}
$$

Write a character to the screen:

$$putChar \qquad :: \quad Char \rightarrow IO \; ()$$
$$putChar \; c \qquad = \quad \dots$$

Write a string to the screen:

$$
\begin{aligned}
putStr \qquad &:: \quad String \rightarrow IO \; () \\
putStr \text{ ""} \qquad &= \quad return \; () \\
putStr \; (x : xs) \qquad &= \quad \textbf{do } putChar \; x \\
&\qquad putStr \; xs
\end{aligned}
$$

Write a string to the screen and move to a new line:

$$
\begin{aligned}
putStrLn \qquad &:: \quad String \rightarrow IO \; () \\
putStrLn \; xs \qquad &= \quad \textbf{do } putStr \; xs \\
&\qquad putChar \text{ '\textbackslash n'}
\end{aligned}
$$

Write a value to the screen:

$$
\begin{aligned}
print \qquad &:: \quad Show \; a \Rightarrow a \rightarrow IO \; () \\
print \qquad &= \quad putStrLn \circ show
\end{aligned}
$$

Display an error message and terminate the program:

$$error \qquad :: \quad String \rightarrow a$$
$$error \; xs \qquad = \quad \dots$$

Symbol table

In this appendix we present a table that summarises the meaning of each of the special Haskell symbols that are used in this book, and shows how each of the symbols is typed using a normal keyboard.

Symbol	Meaning	Typed
→	maps to	->
⇒	class constraint	=>
≥	at least	>=
≤	at most	<=
≠	inequality	/=
∧	conjunction	&&
∨	disjunction	||
¬	negation	not
↑	exponentiation	^
∘	composition	.
λ	abstraction	\
++	append	++
←	drawn from	<-
⋙	sequencing	>>=
+++	choice	+++

Bibliography

1. Richard Bird and Oege de Moor. *Algebra of Programming*. Prentice Hall, 1997.
2. Richard Bird and Shin-Cheng Mu. Countdown: A Case Study in Origami Programming. University of Oxford, 2005.
3. Richard Bird and Philip Wadler. *An Introduction to Functional Programming*. Prentice Hall, 1988.
4. Koen Claessen and John Hughes. QuickCheck: A Lightweight Tool for Random Testing of Haskell Programs. In *Proceedings of the Fifth ACM SIGPLAN International Conference on Functional Programming*, Montreal, Canada, September 2000.
5. Nils Anders Danielsson and Patrik Jansson. Chasing Bottoms: A Case Study in Program Verification in the Presense of Partial and Infinite Values. In *Proceedings of the 7th International Conference on Mathematics of Program Construction*, volume 3125 of *Lecture Notes in Computer Science*, Stirling, Scotland, Springer, 2004.
6. Karl-Filip Faxén. A Static Semantics for Haskell. In Graham Hutton, editor, *Journal of Functional Programming, Special Double Issue on Haskell*, **12**(4&5). Cambridge University Press, 2002.
7. Jeremy Gibbons and Oege de Moor, eds. *The Fun of Programming*. Palgrave, 2003.
8. Jeremy Gibbons and Graham Hutton. Proof Methods for Corecursive Programs. *Fundamenta Informaticae: Special Issue on Program Transformation*, **66**(4): 353–366, 2005.
9. Andy Gill and Simon Marlow. Happy: A Parser Generator for Haskell. Available on the web from: www.haskell.org/happy.
10. Hugh Glaser, Pieter Hartel, and Paul Garratt. Programming by Numbers: A Programming Method for Novices. *The Computer Journal*, **43**(4), 2000.
11. Paul Hudak. Conception, Evolution and Application of Functional Programming Languages. *Communications of the ACM*, **21**(3): 359–411, 1989.
12. Gerard Huet. The Zipper. *Journal of Functional Programming*, **7**(5): 549–554, September 1997.
13. John Hughes. Why Functional Programming Matters. *The Computer Journal*, **32**(2): 98–107, 1989.
14. Graham Hutton. A Tutorial on the Universality and Expressiveness of Fold. *Journal of Functional Programming*, **9**(4): 355–372, 1999.
15. Graham Hutton. The Countdown Problem. *Journal of Functional Programming*, **12**(6): 609–616, 2002.
16. Graham Hutton and Erik Meijer. Monadic Parser Combinators. Technical Report NOTTCS-TR-96-4, Department of Computer Science, University of Nottingham, 1996.

17. Graham Hutton and Erik Meijer. Monadic Parsing in Haskell. *Journal of Functional Programming*, **8**(4): 437–444, 1998.

18. Graham Hutton and Joel Wright. Compiling Exceptions Correctly. In *Proceedings of the 7th International Conference on Mathematics of Program Construction*, vol. 3125 of *Lecture Notes in Computer Science*, Stirling, Scotland. Springer, 2004.

19. Graham Hutton and Joel Wright. Calculating an Exceptional Machine. In Hans-Wolfgang Loidl, ed., *Trends in Functional Programming, vol. 5*: Intellect, February 2006. Selected papers from the Fifth Symposium on Trends in Functional Programming, Munich, November 2004.

20. Mark P. Jones. Typing Haskell in Haskell. In *Proceedings of the 1999 Haskell Workshop*, Paris, France, 1999.

21. John Launchbury. A Natural Semantics for Lazy Evaluation. In *Proceedings of the 20th ACM SIGPLAN-SIGACT Symposium on Principles of Programming Languages*, pages 144–154, Charleston, South Carolina, January 1993.

22. Daan Leijen. Parsec: A Parsing Library for Haskell. Available on the web from: `www.haskell.org/parsec`.

23. Saunders MacLane. *Categories for the Working Mathematician*. Number 5 in *Graduate Texts in Mathematics*. Springer-Verlag, 1971.

24. Simon Peyton Jones. Tackling the Awkward Squad: Monadic Input/Output, Concurrency, Exceptions, and Foreign-Language Calls in Haskell. In Tony Hoare, Manfred Broy, and Ralf Steinbruggen, eds., *Engineering Theories of Software Construction*, pages 47–96. IOS Press, 2001. Presented at the 2000 Marktoberdorf Summer School.

25. Simon Peyton Jones. *Haskell 98 Language and Libraries: The Revised Report*. Cambridge University Press, 2003. Also available on the web from `www.haskell.org/definition`.

26. Simon Peyton Jones and David Lester. *Implementing Functional Languages: A Tutorial*. Prentice Hall, 1992.

27. V.J. Rayward-Smith. *A First Course in Formal Language Theory*, vol. 234 of *Pitman Research Notes in Math*. Blackwell Scientific Publications, 1983.

28. John C. Reynolds. *Theories of Programming Languages*. Cambridge University Press, 1998.

29. Simon Singh. *The Code Book: The Secret History of Codes and Code Breaking*. Fourth Estate, 1999.

30. Philip Wadler. The Concatenate Vanishes. University of Glasgow, 1989.

31. Philip Wadler. Monads for Functional Programming. In Manfred Broy, ed., *Proceedings of the Marktoberdorf Summer School on Program Design Calculi*. Springer–Verlag, 1992.

Index